September 25–October 31, 1986
The Temple Gallery
Temple University
Tyler School of Art
Philadelphia, PA

Exhibition Curated
by Julie Courtney

Editor: Avery Rome

Project Manager: Anell Alexander

Design and Production: Tyler Design Workshop—Frank Baseman, Margaret Pak

Printing: Tyler Offset Workshop—Michael Becotte

Photography: Principal **DARING** Photographer—Tom Levy

Additional Photography— ARTPARK Photographers, Lewiston, NY, 1975, 1976, 1986; Thomas Beck; Neil Benson; Lois Johnson; John Kosmer; Tom Levy; Phil Simkin.

PHILLIPS SIMKIN is published to accompany an exhibition organized by The Temple Gallery, Temple University, Philadelphia, PA and is funded in part by the National Endowment for the Arts and the Pennsylvania Council on the Arts.

Library of Congress Number: 87-50354
ISBN: 0-939351-01-3

TABLE OF CONTENTS

ACKNOWLEDGMENTS

Julie Courtney
Director, The Temple Gallery
Temple University,
Tyler School of Art

Any exhibition depends on the support and encouragement of many organizations and individuals. I extend my most sincere appreciation to the National Endowment for the Arts and the Pennsylvania Council on the Arts. Without their financial support and their votes of confidence, this project would have not been so daring! I am grateful to Peter J. Liacouras, President of Temple University for his ongoing support of our exhibition program.

Many thanks to Phil Simkin for his hard work in putting together such a grandiose project. I am also indebted to my Assistant Director, Anell Alexander, who also acted as Project Director for **DARING** and coordinated the endless details of the exhibition and the catalogue.

Special thanks to Frank Baseman, Director, Tyler Design Workshop, who designed the catalogue, and to Avery Rome, who edited all of the written material. Both of these jobs were monumental and they are both to be congratulated.

As I have stated before, artistic collaboration is one of the key ingredients to a successful Simkin project. M. R. Daniels, Scott Roper and the staff of S.M.R.D. Theatricals took a seemingly impossible fantasy and turned it into a beautiful reality. I applaud their hard work and professionalism. Tom Levy did an excellent job documenting even the most minute details of **DARING** and we appreciate his commitment to the project. I am particularly grateful to Lois Johnson who helped me to keep things in perspective and to add a sense of humor when I was losing mine. The many artists and property owners who donated their time and expertise deserve our thanks. Sue Squires, Connie Coleman, Alan Powell and Joe D'Agostino contributed significantly to the success of the project. Thanks to photographer Neil Benson and designer Mary Phelan for their work on the announcement.

We celebrated our one year anniversary during the **DARING** installation. My thanks to Bunny Glick, Eleanor Tarbox, Miriam Mednick Rothman, Helen and Jack Bershad, Barbara and Ted Aronson, Eileen Rosenau, Howard Caspar and Gene and Debby Lefevre for their help in making the celebration a success!

Many people at Temple University gave their help, advice and encouragement. Thanks to Acting Vice President Robert G. Scanlon for his understanding. My thanks to Tyler's Dean George Bayliss and Temple Center City's Director, Gillian Gilhool for their continued support. John Higgins and Jack Petrie from Physical Planning gave us technical advice; Irene Tasca from OCIS recommended vendors from whom we borrowed equip-

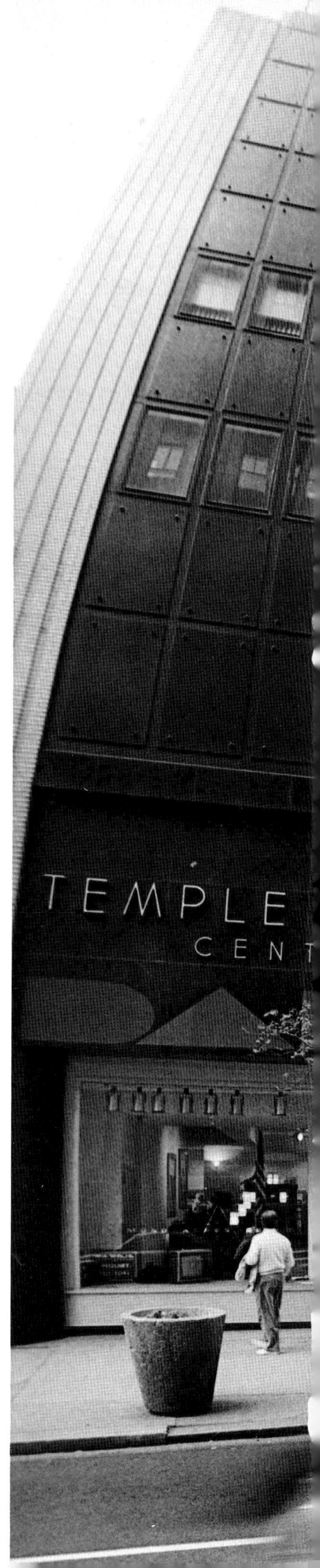

DARING Tower at 1619 Walnut Street.

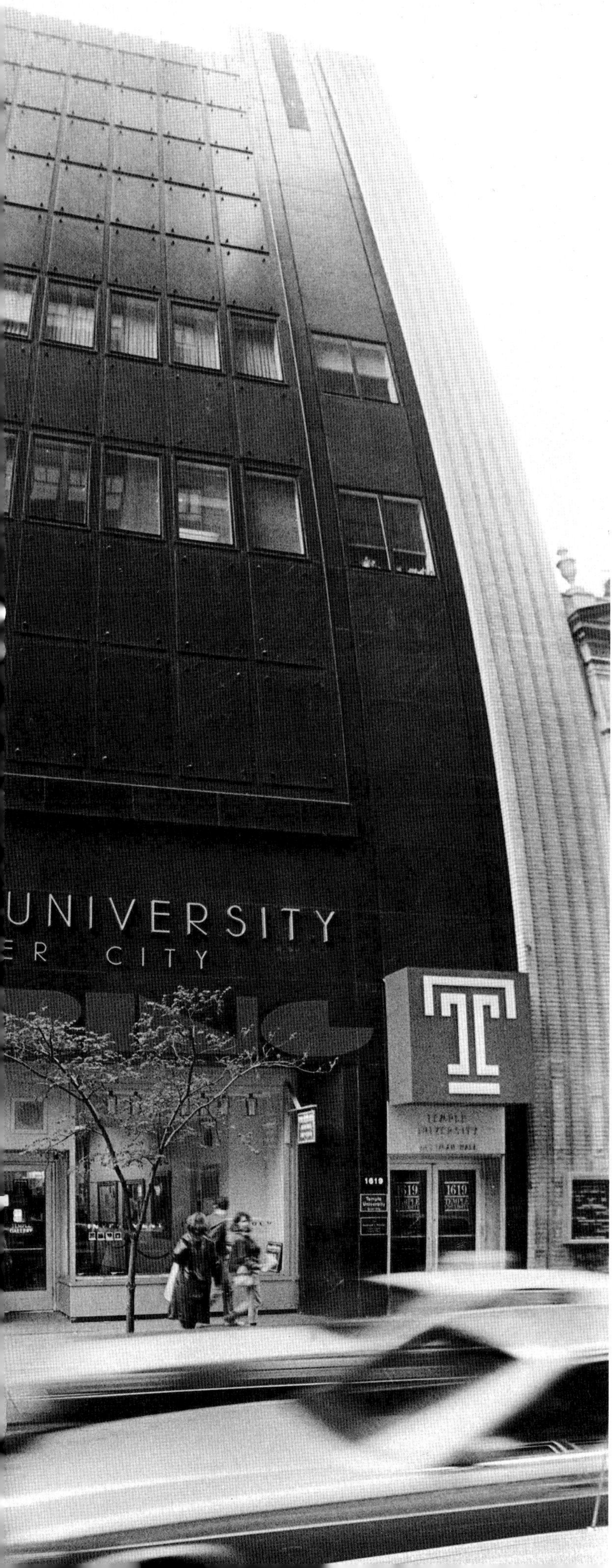

ment; Richard Smith, Elsie Roberts and Phyllis Smith of Research and Program Development assisted with our grants. Marvin Hill and James Johnson of TUCC Media Services, Eleanor Myers of the General Counsel's office, and Linda Fields from Public Information were all generous in giving their time and suggestions and we couldn't have done this without their help. Special thanks to Sarah Chapman of Conwell Dance Lab for her enthusiasm and her recommendation of the four dancers who performed at the opening: Philip Grosser, Will Chapman, Betty Lee and Connie Vandarakis.

Special appreciation goes to my staff who worked so hard on the many details of this project. Graduate Assistants Richard Harvey and Ursula Hawlitschka contributed enormously to the many aspects of the installation and projects which followed. Student workers David Hunter, Gail Goldner, Heather Callaghan, Maria Fogman, Margie Gilbert, Kim Hornberger and Anthony Newkirk all participated as monitors and performed tasks above and beyond the call of duty.

INTRODUCTION

By Julie Courtney

When Phil Simkin came to me with a proposal entitled *Bagels, Bialys and Bleach* two years ago, The Temple Gallery was merely architectural drawings on paper. It seemed like a proposal worth pursuing—until the Gallery was actually finished, and then it was so beautifully and elegantly designed by Venturi, Rauch and Scott Brown that I couldn't bear the thought of laundry detergent smelling up our pristine new space while the washing machine overflowed, ruining the floor. As politely as I could, I suggested that Phil make another proposal. He very good-naturedly pulled out of his pocket a brief proposal for a real estate venture. That seemed more appropriate, more "eighties" to me. The laundromat-gallery-cafe had also been an old fantasy of mine in the seventies—I had grown up.

Thus **DARING** was born. **DARING (Diamond Acres Real(i)ty Investment Network Group)**, is a real estate venture whose name "Diamond Acres" was based on Temple University's founder Russell Conwell's famous "Acres of Diamonds" speech. It somehow seemed more comfortable for the Gallery. Phil is an alumnus of Temple's Tyler School of Art, and it seemed appropriate for this native son to kick off our first full season with an extravagant project on such a timely subject. Since Phil had just purchased a new home in South Philadelphia he was well versed in 'real estate speak' and I was feeling fairly fluent in 'grant speak,' so we sat down at the computer and fed in a mixture of our respective 'languages.' This resulted in our receiving generous grants from both the National Endowment for the Arts and the Pennsylvania Council on the Arts. Private donors emerged as well. **DARING** was to become a reality.

The premise was to inventory 'properties' that interested people would donate to **DARING** and to make these spaces available to artists who wished to propose temporary works for them. The properties ranged from back yards to storefront windows to planters to garage doors to shells and summer camps. The projects proposed included performances, window installations, mural paintings and sculpture. The whole concept was intended to give young or underexposed artists an opportunity to exercise their creativity in order to produce experimental works.

DARING was to be the fifth project in Phil's **American Enterprise Series.** The Temple Gallery was to function, on one level, as an actual real estate office. The very nature of Phil's work is usually site specific, temporary and humorous. In the case of **DARING,** the design and details of the real estate office would mimic the design of the Gallery which had been so carefully planned by the architects of the space. The underlying assumption was that Simkin's plans would respond to the existing interior architecture, and where appropriate, parody it. The Gallery was to 'disappear' so that **DARING** could debut with complete believability. Documentation of the first four of Phil's 'enterprises' **(Philston; Institute for Advanced Creative Thoughts and Stuff,** or **IFACTS: Arts and Cultural Maintenance Engineers Implementing New Creations,** or **ACME, INC.**; and **Cable Knitted News,** or **CKN)** would decorate the walls of the real estate office.

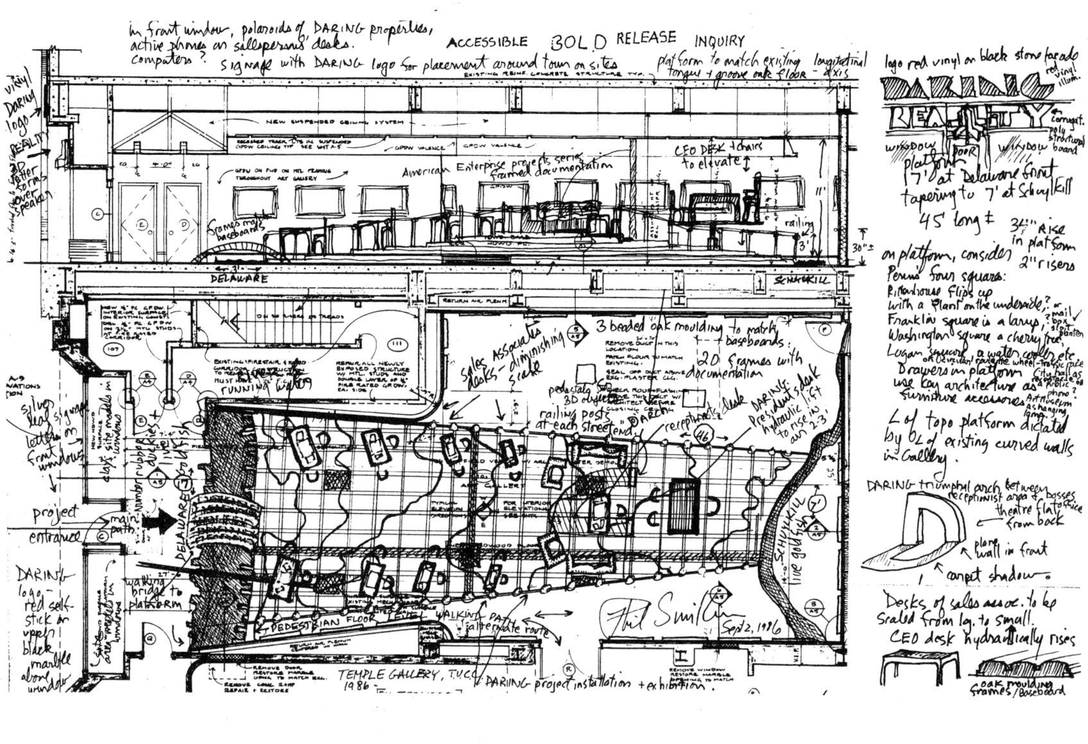

"Architectural Drawing" of DARING installation by Phil Simkin

An important element in Phil's work (and most appealing to me) is his collaboration with other artists. Sculptor Barbara Ansell was given the assignment to build the frames for the project documentation which Phil was to create. Phil's attention to detail was so precise he had the manufacturers of Venturi's eccentric baseboards mill the same red oak beaded board for the frames. Though compulsive and labor intensive, the effect was brilliant!

Phil's 'architectural drawings' usually consist of bleeding lines of felt pen on a paper napkin. We interviewed several carpenters, and they just shook their heads. When M. R. Daniels of S.M.R.D. Theatricals said that she understood the drawings completely, the deal was sealed, M. R. and her partner Scott Roper are artists who build stage sets, and they performed miracles with **DARING.** This was the ultimate artistic collaboration of the project. Phil worked very closely with them, and it really was remarkable how they translated his food-stained scribbles into the fabulous set that filled the Gallery.

According to Phil's plan, the new 'office' floor was to be wedge shaped, following the Gallery's inwardly canted front walls. It ascended in stepped planes that matched the topographically mapped elevation rises between the two rivers which border Center City Philadelphia. The 'rivers,' at either end of the Gallery, were stocked with gold fish. The wooden inlay floor corresponded to William Penn's gridded street plan which had been shifted so that The Temple Gallery's location was its central attraction. The floor was elevated, creating a change in orientation and perspective so that visitors felt a bit like Alice in Wonderland with their heads just below ceiling level.

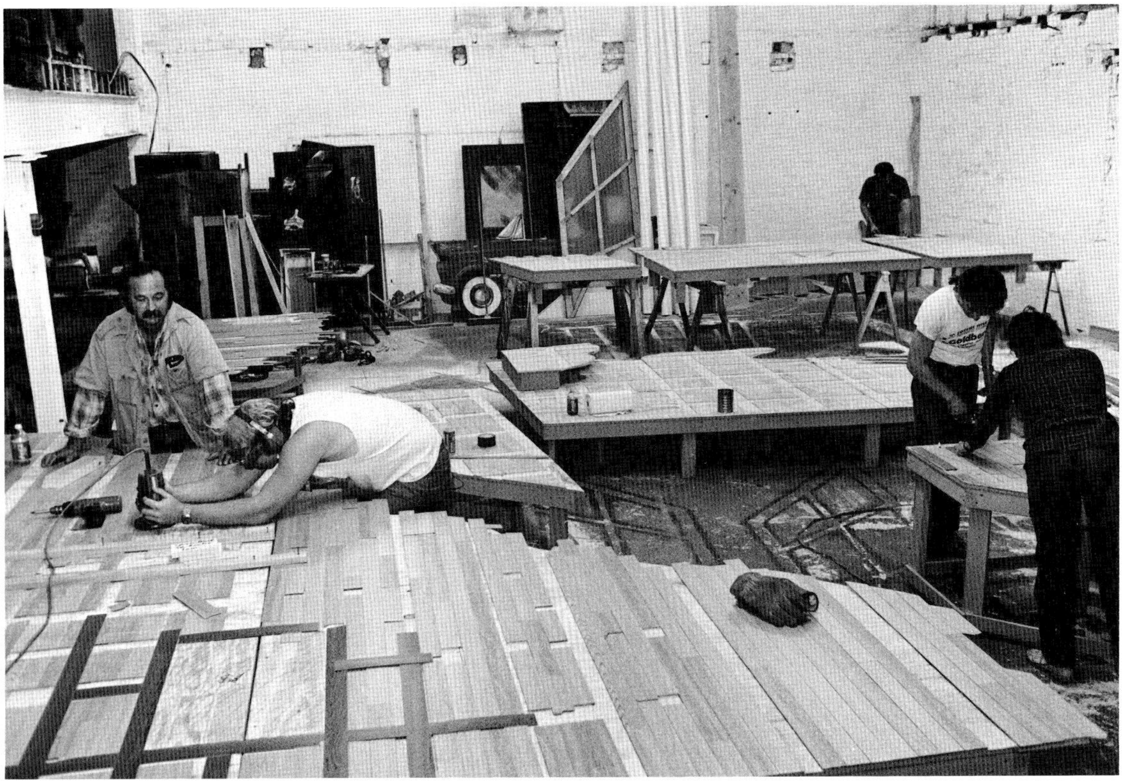

Artist Phil Simkin working with crew at SMRD Theatricals.

On the platform there was an arch with a large D-shaped cut-out which served as the entrance to the boss's 'office.' This was basically Phil's oversized desk. The desk and seated President (Phil) were capable of being cranked up with a hidden jack to within inches of the ceiling, carrying the President to the 'top of the corporate ladder' in a more literal way than one usually imagines.

Three-foot-tall red vinyl letters of the **DARING** logo were adhered to the Gallery's facade. The windows were painstakingly silver leafed with the entire corporate name, **Diamond Acres Real[i]ty Investment Network Group**, by artist Sue Squires which gave the enterprise credibility. Her daily appearance in the window before we opened became a preliminary performance component to the main event.

Other elements of real[i]ty included real estate signs silk screen printed by Laurel Schwass of Philadelphia Colleges of the Arts' Printmaking Shop. These signs included, of course, the **DARING** logo with the Gallery's phone number and words that provided 'realty' inferences with 'reality' references: BOLD, ACCESSIBLE, INFORMATIVE, RELEASE, INQUIRY. We selected the ACCESSIBLE sign for the front window as it reflected the mission of The Temple Gallery. The signs were also displayed on the donated properties to mark **DARING's** presence around the city.

Overhead fabrication view of DARING Philadelphia city street floor inlay at SMRD workshop.

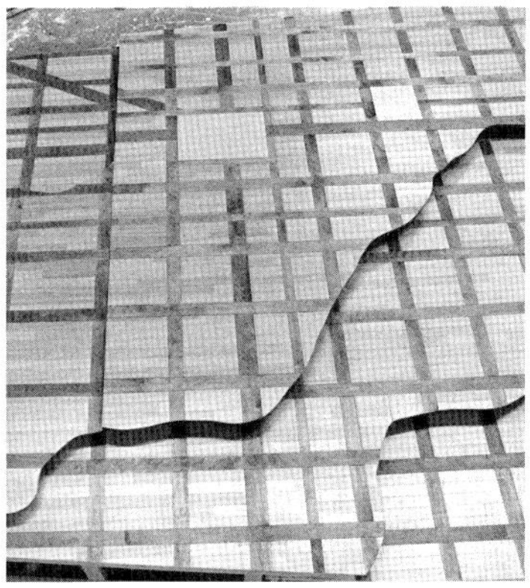

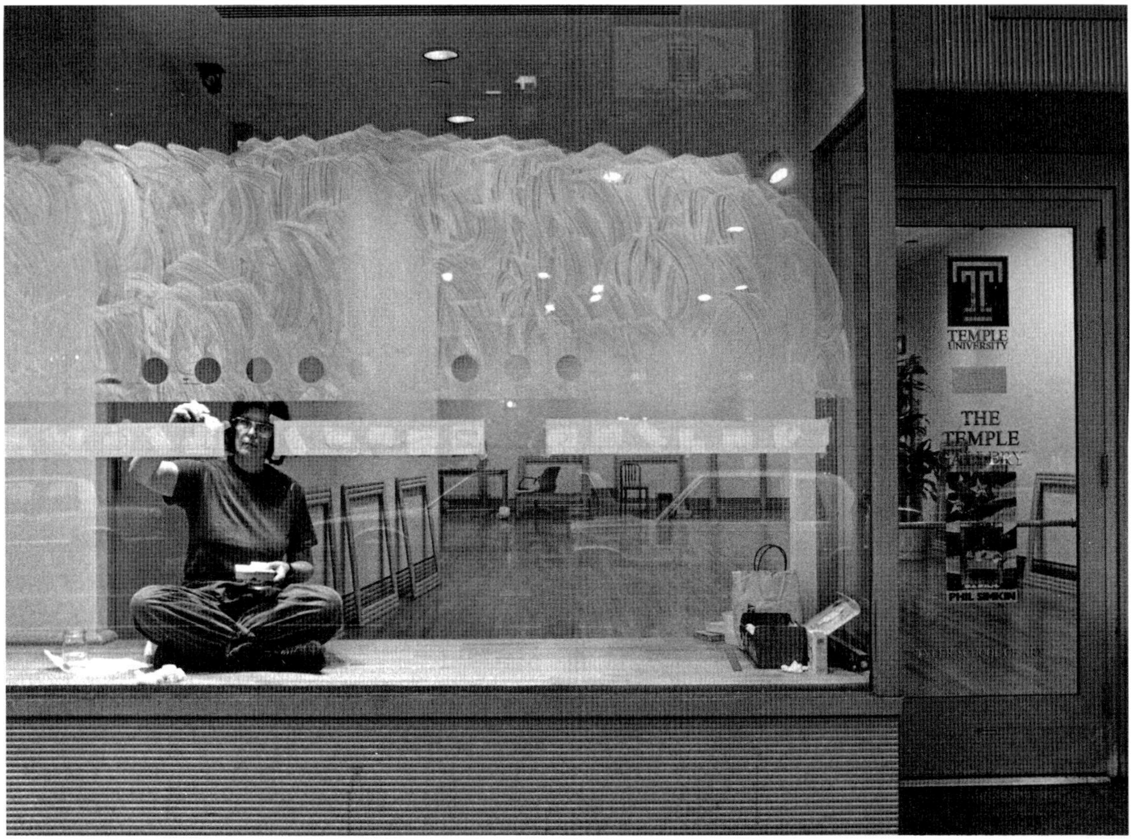

Philadelphia artist Sue Squires silver leafs "Diamond Acres Real(i)ty Investment Network Group" on the storefront window of The Temple Gallery.

Just before the opening of **DARING** at The Temple Gallery, Phil created a 'field office' at Fleisher Art Memorial which served as his contribution to an exhibition of the Challenge jurors' works. This preview helped to acquire properties and to alert local artists of what was about to take place.

To further publicize the venture, Phil commissioned video artists Connie Coleman and Alan Powell to create a television commercial. Phil as the huckster made his sales pitch interspersed with shots of the available properties. The commercial played every day, all day long on a monitor that was placed in the Gallery's window. Joe D'Agostino, a local composer and video producer, also became involved. He provided the background music for the commercial and composed the music to Phil's lyrics for the "DARING Ditty." This also was heard all day in the 'office.'

Other artists were enlisted. James Drew manufactured embroidered patches with the **DARING** logo, which were sewn onto red Temple blazers, much in the fashion of Century 21 realtors. Jeanette McGrath made a paper lamp in the shape of the Philadelphia Museum of Art that hung in the appropriate place on the topographic map. Romayne DuPraw tended the goldfish and added some aquatic sculptural constructions of her own as habitats for the undersea life. The office was stylishly outfitted with all the accoutrements of any new business: **DARING** stationery and business cards with Phil's graphic design, eight desks customized and built by the S.M.R.D. crew, and finishing accessories courtesy of IKEA. Phil had called IKEA on a lark, and their public relations director, Phran Novelli, thought that the project sounded intriguing. They were extremely generous and let Phil go on a fantasy shopping spree. IKEA showed up just before the details were complete and in addition loaned him furniture including a red leather couch, which gave the 'office' the kind of class Phil had hoped to achieve.

From day one, constantly on hand to document every move, was Phil's friend, Tom Levy, who we dubbed Court Photographer. Tom has worked with Phil for years and many of Tom's photographs documenting past **American Enterprise Series** projects were incorporated into Phil's drawings to decorate the company's walls.

Gallery openings are usually 'photo finish,' and this project was no exception. Only minutes before the 5 o'clock opening time, Assistant Director Anell Alexander and crew completed the installation of the accompanying works of art. Phil was under the set, making sure that everything was plugged in and all the lights were on. The effect was beautiful and professional—and convincing. Many people believed that the Gallery had actually disappeared and had been replaced by a new business.

The opening was exciting, with Phil arriving in a white stretch limousine. Four dancers from Temple's Conwell Dance Lab, choreographed an hommage to **DARING** and created a sensation while performing first outside in the rain and then inside on the multi-level stage set. No one fell, to my great relief, and the dancers hammed it up in a way appropriately exaggerated for any Simkin event. The Gallery and sidewalk were packed and street traffic came to a standstill. For Phil all of the most coveted aspects of public art were in simultaneous operation—lots of happy people and lots of interaction.

The success of the evening seemed to ripple through the five weeks of the project. In the subsequent month, properties were donated and proposals were made. Phil and I weeded out the impossible spaces and projects, and in the end we came up with 28 properties and 32 proposals. We matched those that seemed appropriate and waited for the return of the 'official' forms we supplied.

Only a few of the projects could be executed before weather made it impossible. Others are being carried out at this writing, and it is hoped that new ones will emerge.

Lynn Denton enacted a performance piece one cold evening on a donated backyard on Rodman Street. With lit candles and a tape recording of her own monologue, she was costumed and blindfolded as she painted primitive icons in white paint on a blue wall. It was a ritualistic multi-media performance piece. The reaction of the neighbors was mixed, as one might expect, but many participated and enjoyed it.

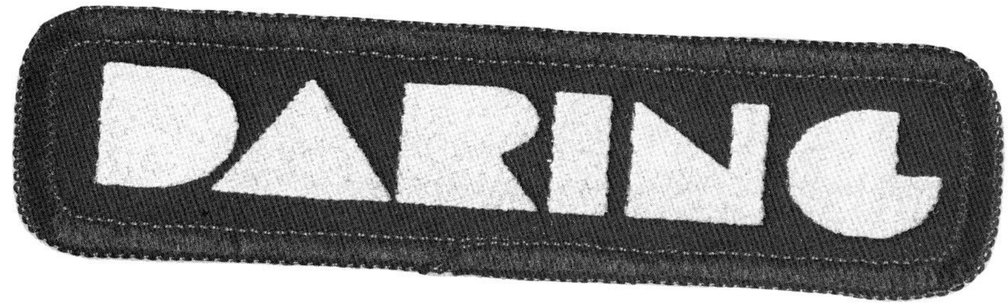

Anell Alexander created a full scale fabric installation that responded to a multi-paned storefront window at Tenth and South Street. She filled the large display area with 35 16-by-14 inch boards, each of which listed the name of a different artist or significant influence in light gray block letters. In the center of each board was a rectangular swatch of fabric that matched the persona of those named. For example, Phil was portrayed with a green flannel plaid.

Other site specific **DARING** installations as described by drawn proposals are anticipated for warmer weather. In a garage shed in suburban Philadelphia, Ann Reichlin plans to construct a piece using natural materials that will change with the elements. John Riley Strockbine proposes a performance involving musicians for a community garden on historic Mole Street.

Phil's fantasy 'enterprise' satisfied my personal artistic mission—to bring art to the "People"—to make them trip over it or walk right into it if necessary. I've always felt that if people were exposed to high art more often, they would learn to appreciate it and to enjoy it. Phil's installation was so eccentric that people came into the Gallery just to see what was going on. Many were surprised to learn that this, too, was art. We gave opportunities to many unknown artists to create works out there on the street, perhaps linking them with patrons, and therefore tightening the art community in Philadelphia.

At the same time we gave the public a chance to experience the spontaneity of art—the delight of discovering something that you're not quite sure of, and of course the opportunity to formally experience Phil Simkin and his unique mind and artmaking genius.

I hope that the success of this project continues past its official closing date of June 30, 1987, and that artists and property owners will continue to work together, "daring" to make available small cultural surprises around and for the city.

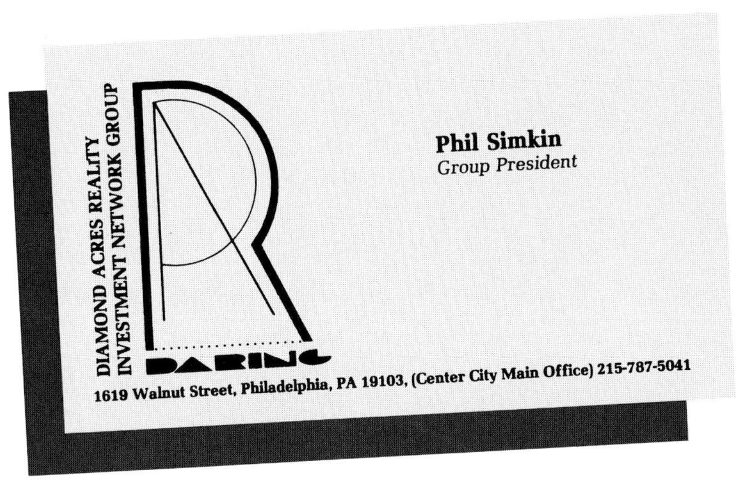

IS IT OR ISN'T IT A REAL ESTATE OFFICE?

By Harriet Senie,
Director of Museum Studies, City College, The City University of New York. Art historian, art critic.

"Is it or isn't it a real estate office?" the cab driver asked in some confusion. "I mean, can you rent an apartment here?" His perplexity was shared by some 100-200 daily visitors who, in one way or another, participated in Phil Simkin's *DARING* installation at The Temple Gallery from September 25-October 31, 1986.

The premise of **DARING—(Diamond Acres Real(i)ty Investment Network Group)**—revolved around real estate, expectations related to 'real' property and puns on 'reality.' By focusing on real estate Simkin zeroed in on a central preoccupation in contemporary life.

DARING transformed the Gallery into a mock real estate office with a real function. The real estate transactions facilitated by **DARING,** however, were not inspired by need or greed. Rather, individuals offered to donate property (space of any sort) for the creation of temporary works of art and artists proposed temporary projects—including performances for these properties. The function of the Gallery, with Simkin acting as broker and Group President of **DARING,** was to match up the two.

Plans for the actual execution of the proposed artist participation pieces were still underway at the time of this writing but, regardless of the outcome, **DARING** set out to fill a very real need. **DARING** was created as part parody and part utility in order to provide young artists with the opportunity to make art in unconventional settings for different audiences. Conversely, the project was designed to provide the viewers with the opportunity to see art in places other than galleries. Simkin hoped that **DARING** might serve as a pilot for future projects, which could perhaps be administered by a municipal program.

The motivation for **DARING,** as for all of his projects, came from what Simkin calls his "endless fascination with human behavior." He is something of a playful 'enfant terrible,' but one who, with the unnerving instinct of a child, goes directly to the heart of an issue. His approach born of the Sixties is basically anti-bureaucratic. Simkin makes art that relates, in the most direct way possible, to life.

He had recently bought a brownstone in South Philadelphia, although he has had his studio in the Philadelphia area since high school. In **DARING,** the artist's

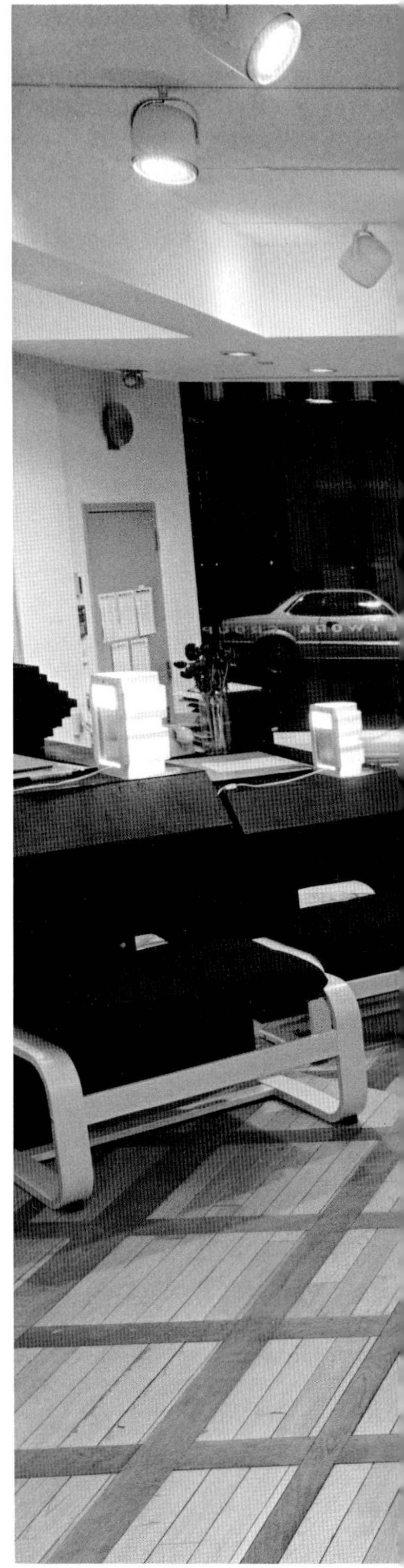

Installation view of DARING from sales associate's desk.

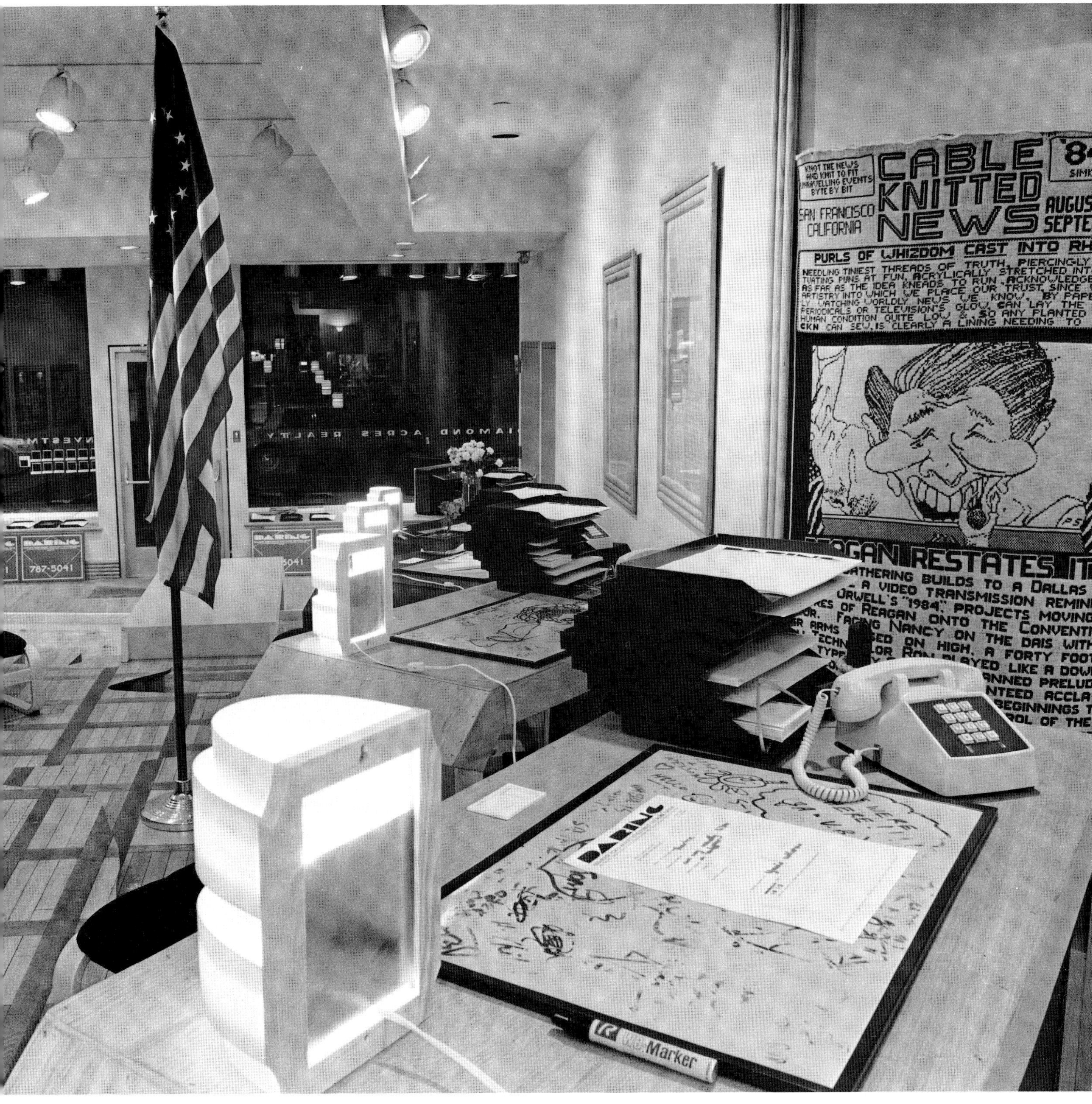
KNOT THE NEWS AND KNIT TO FIT UNRAVELLING EVENTS BYTE BY BIT
CABLE KNITTED NEWS
SAN FRANCISCO CALIFORNIA
787-5041
Marker

thoughts about and experiences with real estate and bureaucracy merged.

The title of the exhibition related directly to the site; it was taken from the "Acres of Diamonds" speech made by Russell Conwell, founder of Temple University. Conwell said, in essence, that you can search the world over for diamonds yet find them in your own backyard. (For Simkin, this philosophy is also applicable to the Philadelphia art world which suffers from an ongoing "cultural identity crisis.")

In designing this exhibition Simkin responded to the brand new gallery space designed by Venturi, Rauch and Scott Brown. The frames for the wall pieces which documented Simkin's other **American Enterprise Series** projects matched the baseboards. The placement of the entire 'office' platform played against the angled walls of the Gallery. The actual complex was built by stage set fabricators, who followed Simkin's initial sketches. There were no shop drawings. Simkin relied on their knowledge and his desire. It was one of the few times that the artist had worked with paid professionals rather than volunteers to execute his installations.

Philadelphia's four main squares were highlighted in orange on the Gallery's topographic floor map. Symbolic elements which related to the history of each square were placed within these areas. A souvenir statue of William Penn stood atop a vertical dish dispenser ('disherator') to denote City Hall. A telescope represented Rittenhouse Square and an American flag was placed on Washington Square. A lazy Susan for business cards marked Logan Circle. More subtly, a mail letter slot in the floor marked the location of Franklin Square.

Installation of DARING logo on building facade,1619 Walnut Street.

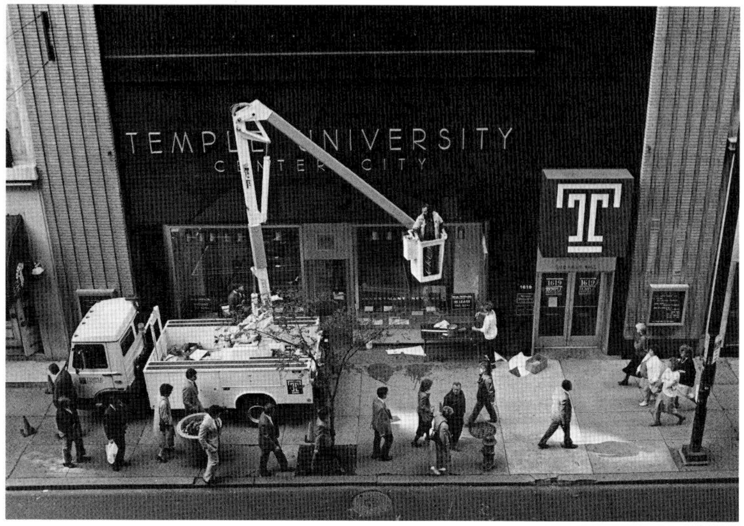

At the front of the 'office' was a bridge spanning a mock Delaware River. The goldfish, fed daily by the artist, generated a murky film comparable to the actual river pollution. A sign at the bridge advised the visitor to, "DARE . . . to proceed at your own risk." The 'office' ended sixty feet later with a similar body of water which represented the Schuylkill River.

At the center of the Gallery/'office' was Group President Simkin's desk, which was designed to be raised and lowered hydraulically as he conducted business. Laminated to the desktop was an aerial view map of Philadelphia. Also prominently displayed on the desk was Simkin's casting of the crack in the Liberty Bell. Simkin had proposed this piece for a public art project in Philadelphia which was never realized. The model was the first and, to this day, the only object of sculpture that the artist ever made, and it is the closest he has ever come to making a permanent piece.

Polaroids of donated properties were posted in the Gallery window, as advertised properties are in a real estate office. Press releases and relevant newspaper articles were also on display. Office furniture which included chairs and custom designed desks outfitted with in-boxes, stationery, blotters, business cards, pencils and telephones were placed on the platform which served as the 'office' floor.

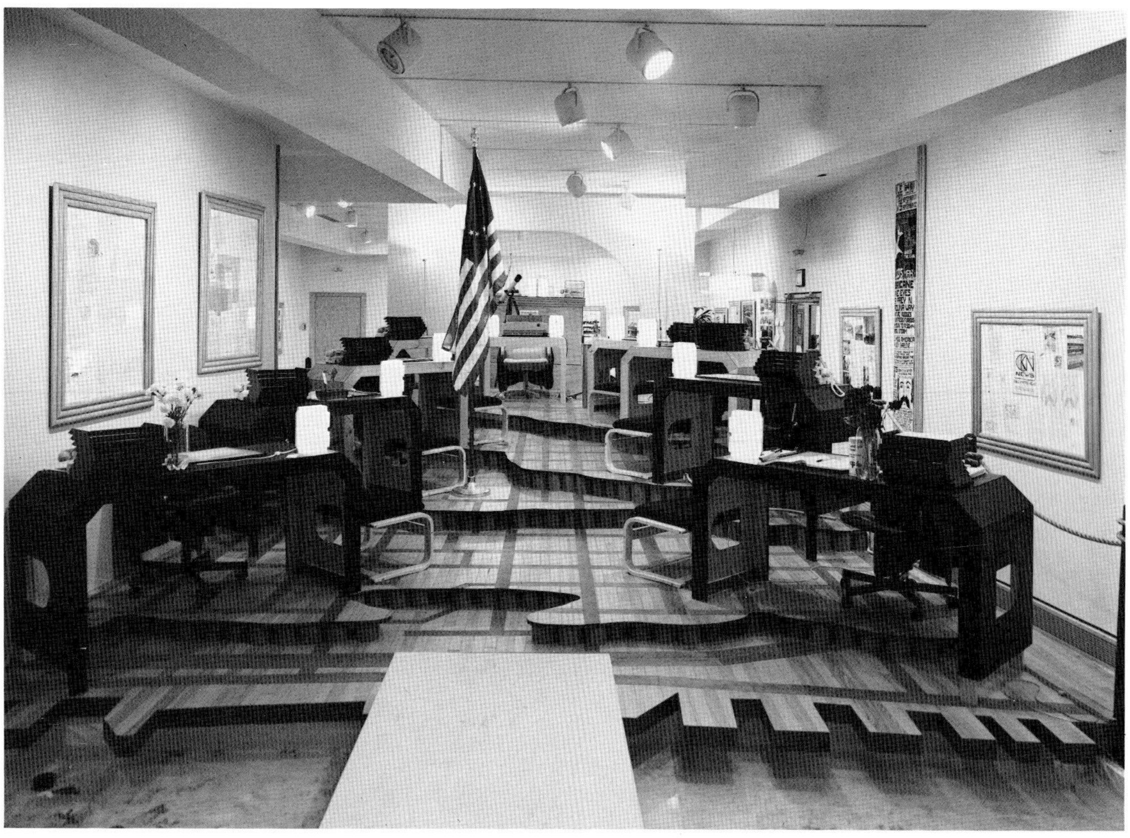

DARING Installation.

Phil Simkin at work with video artists Connie Coleman and Alan Powell and composer Joe D'Agostino.

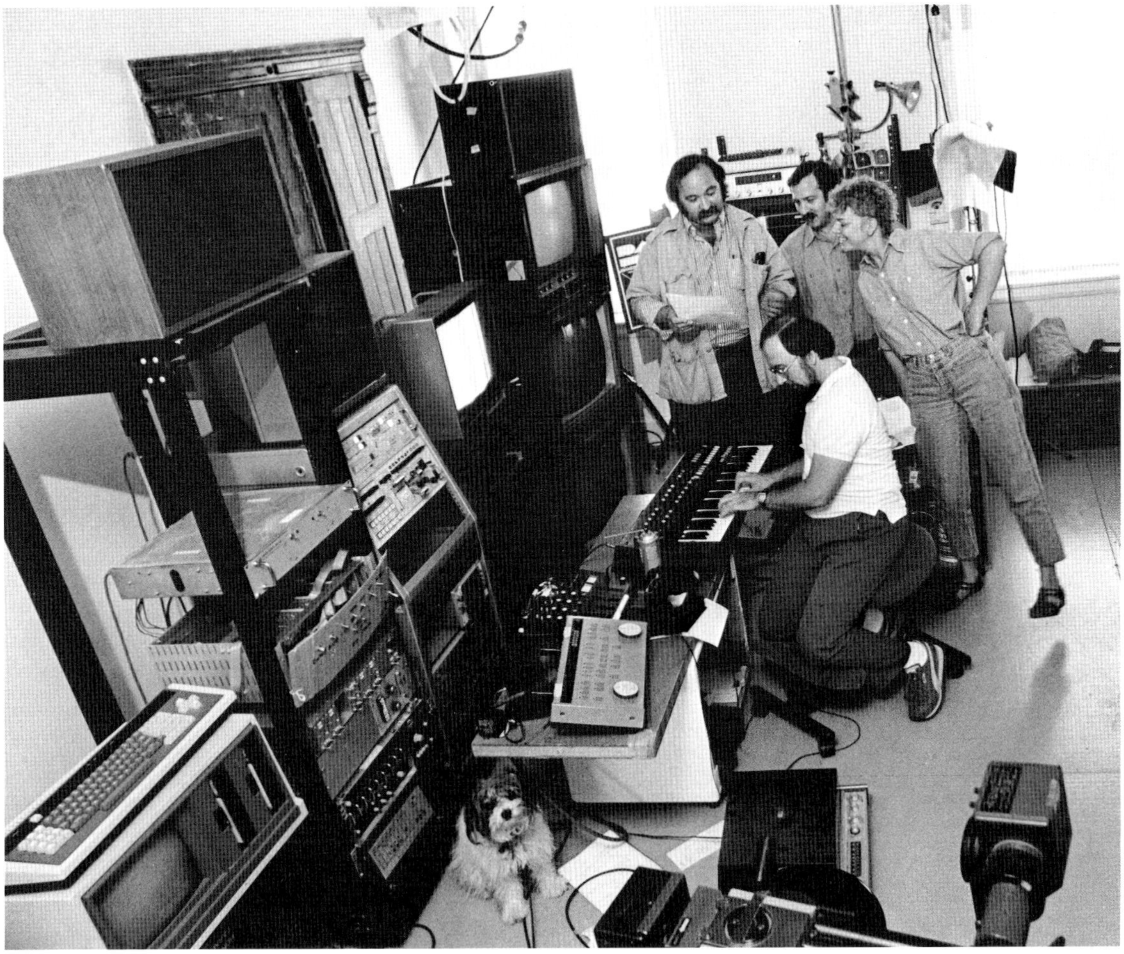

DARING REAL[I]TY DITTY
Lyrics: Phil Simkin
Music: Joe D'Agostino

REFRAIN: We're all playing at
Real-ity
It's clear as the Bell and plain to see
Owning to a plot in this rhyming story
Anticipate your end
for deeded 'round the bend
waits your slot in Glory.

Reality is only space
Definitions of a place
Length times width, "airspace" too!
Location, location, maybe a view?

Plotted measurements, circumscribed
Sight lines most clearly described
Centuries of control over every degree
Earth and turf combo, free or by decree?

Refrain

A volume, a void, Land rights deployed
Occupied, Empty, entitlements enjoyed
Built-up, Torn down, eminent domain
A long term investment or a short term gain

Acquire land quite low
Build up a portfolio
Then sell it high
Profit to the sky
Real-ity's for those in the know

Refrain

Cut interest rates, Oh to shave a point
Professional sincerity, Oh pray to annoint
The whole epitome of dealing in property
is digging tangibility for a set fee

(Slow beat)

Land upon a parcel
Stake a claim to fate
Pay to pile up moments
Till that payoff date

REAL(i)TY SENSITIVE

REAL(i)TY SENSITIVE

Definitive Art-chitecture
Requires Intuitive New Ground
D.A.R.I.N.G.
Diamond Acres you see
My special reality
is partly art
slight parody profound
seeking its moment
in your mind and on the ground
DARING's the new biz around

Deed to DARING your plots
loan us your curbs and lots
lease us your slivers and slots
We're multiple listing our hots:
for leeway land
urban landscape or sand
air rights/riparian sites
left-over edges/ends of ledges
Or most anything that you gots!

If you've some time to spare
Join our enterprise if you dare
Sit at our desks and pursue
acquisition of space with a view
For Arts' sake alone
Blanket Philly by phone
Assemble DARING stone by stone
And we will forge the new:
an aesthetic stew
an artistic brew
conceptual goo
And we will dare to *do*!

Refrain

Creative Personalities
Seize the city's breeze
And propose ideas to visually tease
inventive solutions to place if you please
with our borrowed properties

Refrain

So come and walk on Philly's plateaus
sight Penn's prim plan between your toes
Aerial view its geometry
Straddle streets and squares to see
Role play Real-ity games with me
Join us in DARING, CARING, SHARING, BARING,
Your creative per-son-al-ity . . . !

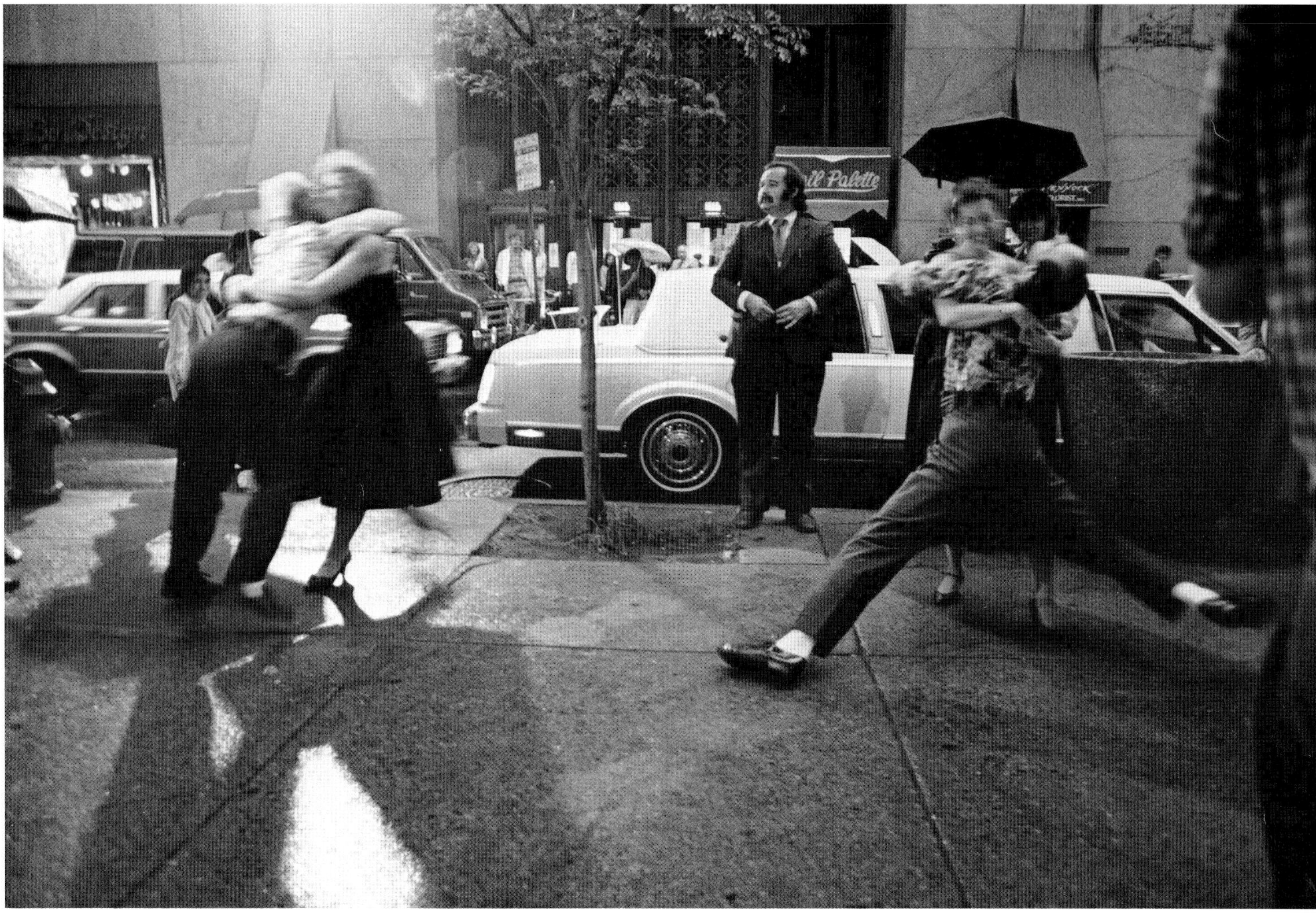

DARING CEO Simkin emerging from stretch limo to the accompaniment of DARING's corps de ballet.

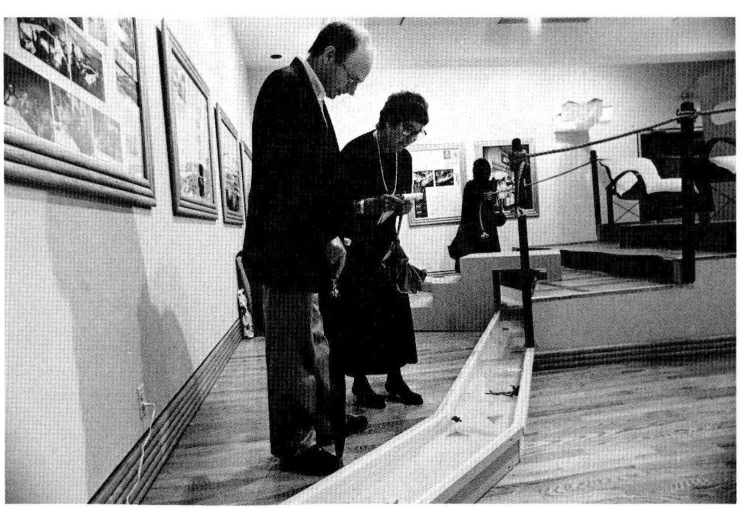

Visitors observe fish and aquatic debris in "Schuylkill River" of DARING installation.

Students, gallery volunteers and the workers manning the desks wore company **DARING** blazers. Signage and costumes were done in red and white, Temple University's colors. The Washington Square flagpole was topped with an owl, the Temple mascot.

Visitors to The Temple Gallery were greeted by a video taped advertisement in the window—in a style reminiscent of a Crazy Eddie commercial—which was shot by video artists Connie Coleman and Alan Powell. The artist as a talking head 'real(i)ty' merchant alternated with vignettes of parcels of odd space donated to the project from all over the city.

Once inside the front door, the Gallery reverberated with a recording of the "DARING Ditty," a thirteen verse song with a repeated refrain. The music for the ditty was composed by Joe D'Agostino and was written and sung by Simkin. Two verses (numbers 6 and 7) were censored as being "real(i)ty sensitive" because they were critical of the University.

DARING was inaugurated by an opening that included a live performance by four Temple dance instructors. Simkin, in full business suit, was delivered to the Gallery in a white limo which remained parked out front for the evening. The four dancers developed one piece for the street in front of the Gallery, which they performed in the rain, and another for the office platform inside. Inside, they danced to the music and lyrics of the "DARING Ditty," which Simkin, who comes from a musical family, sang for the opening night crowd. The opening evolved like a continuous performance event. Providing additional glitz and glamour were three photographers and two video crews. The opening had all of the accoutrements often found at the opening party for any new business. Business, as it were, began almost at once. Joe Rishel, curator of 19th century European art at the Philadelphia Museum of Art and his wife, Museum Director Anne D'Harnoncourt, donated their garage door for a temporary art piece. Others donated properties that included storefront windows, summer camps, and even a set of planters from the Museum of Modern Art's former sculpture garden.

Simkin wanted to acquire Center City properties owned by people who were ready to become involved with his venture. To confirm the deals, he sent letters in legalese to the property owners. Artists could submit proposals directly to **DARING.** These proposals were reviewed by Simkin and the Gallery Director Julie Courtney in order to prevent unsafe, impractical or conceptually inappropriate works. The Gallery then matched artists with properties; the final approval for execution was made by the patron, the donor of the property. Simkin provided an owner agreement form to clinch the deal.

In this process Simkin changed the traditional role of the artist from one of maker to one of planner and facilitator. The artist as entrepreneur is a telling commentary on the business of making art in today's commercial world. During the course of the exhibition the artist sat at his desk in the Gallery and 'worked,' interacting with the public when appropriate. In this social context, the artist became a functioning part of the installation. Interaction with the public has always been an integral part of Simkin's art. However, **DARING** was one of the few times that the artist had entered his scenario in such a direct way.

The run of the exhibition coincided with a strike by Temple faculty for higher wages. At one point, University officials said that the

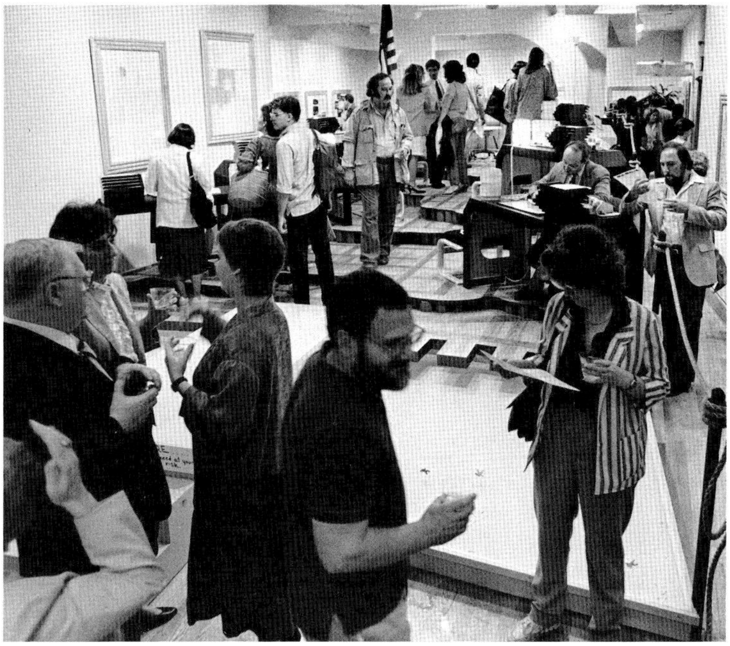

DARING opening night view of "Delaware River" stocked with goldfish, and celebrants considering real(i)ty options similarly reinforced by refreshing liquids.

Opening night crowd.

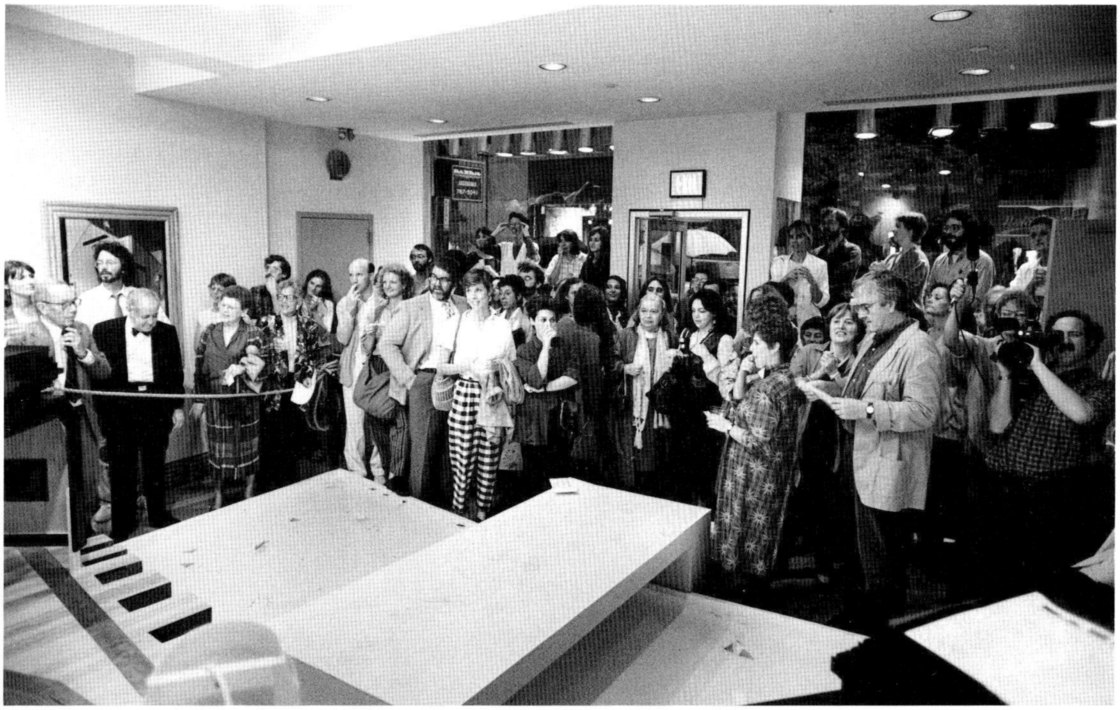

Child enjoying "Delaware River" of **DARING** installation.

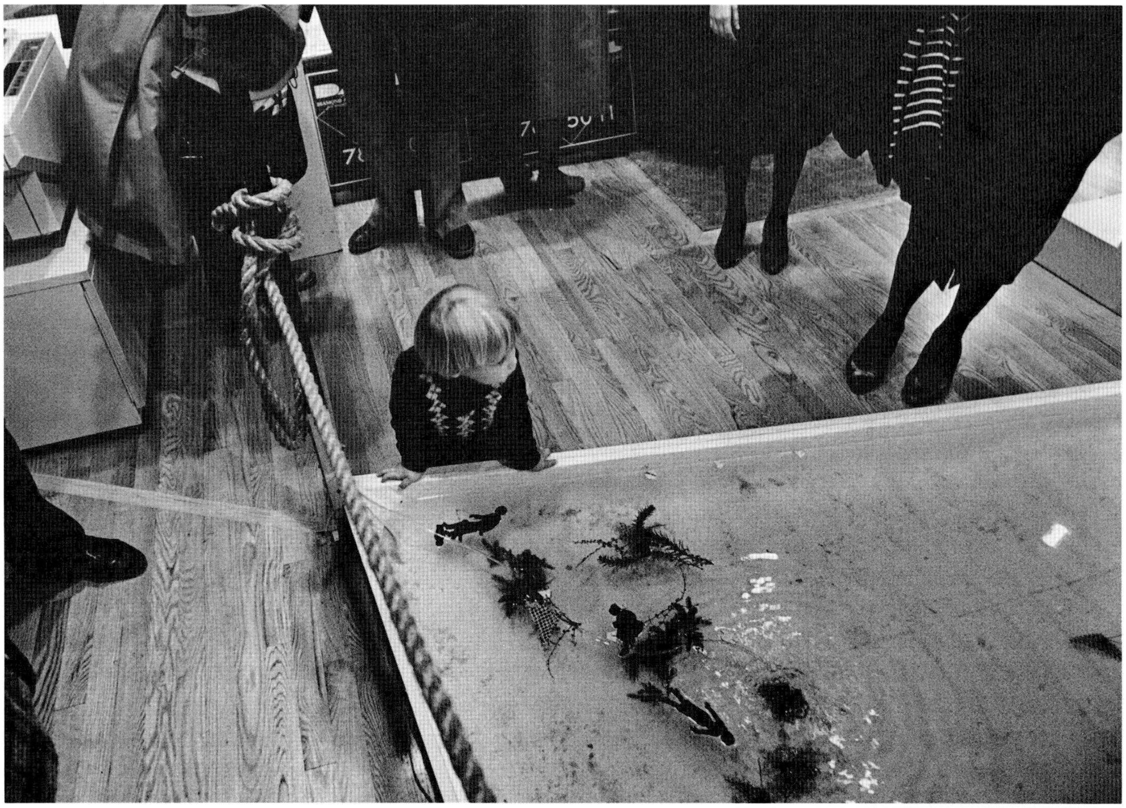

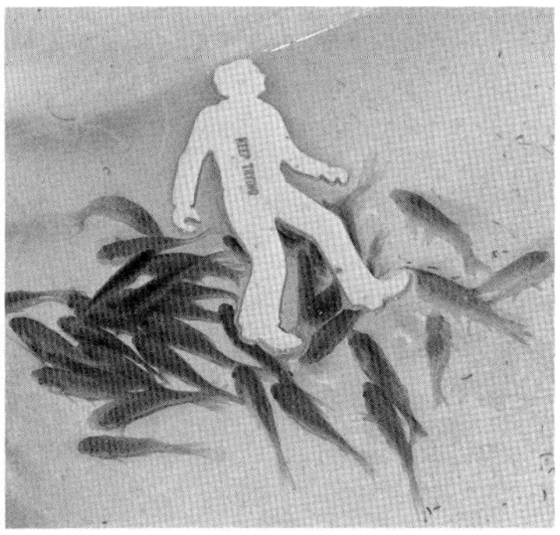

Detail of goldfish in "Delaware River."

DARING signs on the Gallery facade had prompted inquiries as to whether the building was for sale. They ordered the lettering removed.

For Simkin, the issue then became one of the freedom of expression vs. the bureaucracy. Simkin called Anne D'Harnoncourt, Director of the Philadelphia Museum of Art, to enlist her support. She called the President of Temple to express her concern. Simkin also hired a lawyer, who threatened to sue the University. The press was notified, and Simkin was photographed climbing a ladder, trying to protect the red plastic letters which spelled **DARING** that were being taken down by workers on a cherry picker. After the ensuing brouhaha, the University's Vice President of Planning and Operations, consented to let Simkin restore the sign.

On Saturday, October 11th, *The Philadelphia Inquirer* front page headline read, "Artist sees red as his work is dismantled." The AP wire picked up the story, and it ran in approximately thirty newspapers across the country. The following Thursday, October 16th there was a follow-up story with the headline, "A disputed work of art is restored." Such publicity is not unusual for Simkin. Frequently his art elicits unexpected responses that become "part of the history of the project."

DARING once more caught the eye of the media on October 24th. That evening, a TV camera from Channel 6 News (Philadelphia's ABC affiliate) was set up in the gallery. From this location, which was chosen by the cameraman (once a Philadelphia College of Art student), the President of the University, Peter Liacouras, announced

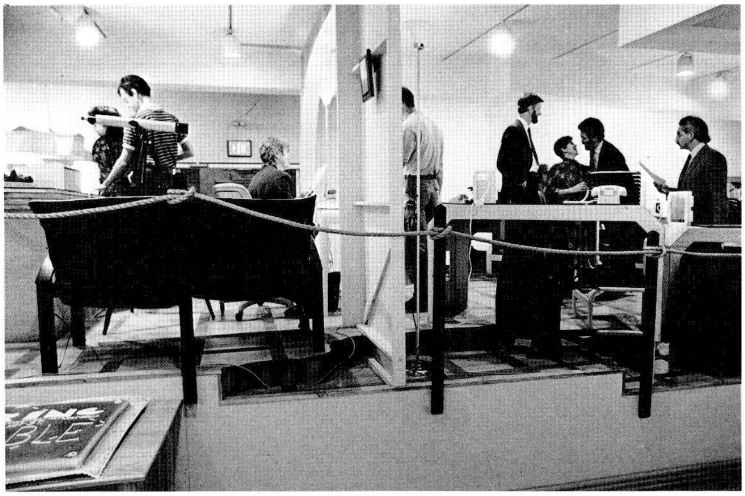

View of **DARING** installation showing multi-level stepped platform, stage set accoutrements and inaugural cake.

that the University's strike had been settled. The artist, who had been dining at a nearby restaurant, was walking by as the lights were being set up. Simkin walked up to Liacouras, shook hands, and introduced himself, saying, "You are now part of the art." Liacouras was even wearing a red tie that matched the office decor. The President responded graciously and apologized for the previous misunderstanding about the exhibition.

Simkin's work is impossible to categorize. He sometimes describes himself as a conceptualist who must see things done. His projects are 'in process' up to the last possible moment. This makes funding difficult since no definitive plan of an installation is available much before the fact. As a result, he has worked more within the institutional system (with university galleries like The Temple Gallery, University of Pennsylvania's Institute of Contemporary Art, and ArtPark) than with commercial galleries or government agencies. He has not sought most of his commissions. Usually he must wait to see who will call next.

Simkin finds nothing unusual in what he does. If anything, he worries that his work "may be too obvious, too conservative." He insists that he's really "a middle class guy—with maybe a touch of Duchamp and a dash of Danny Kaye, a bit of Puck." In the sense that Simkin does not make his art for an elite art audience, this is true. Instead, his focus has been on the social world as it is, the interconnectedness of people and systems, and the foibles of both.

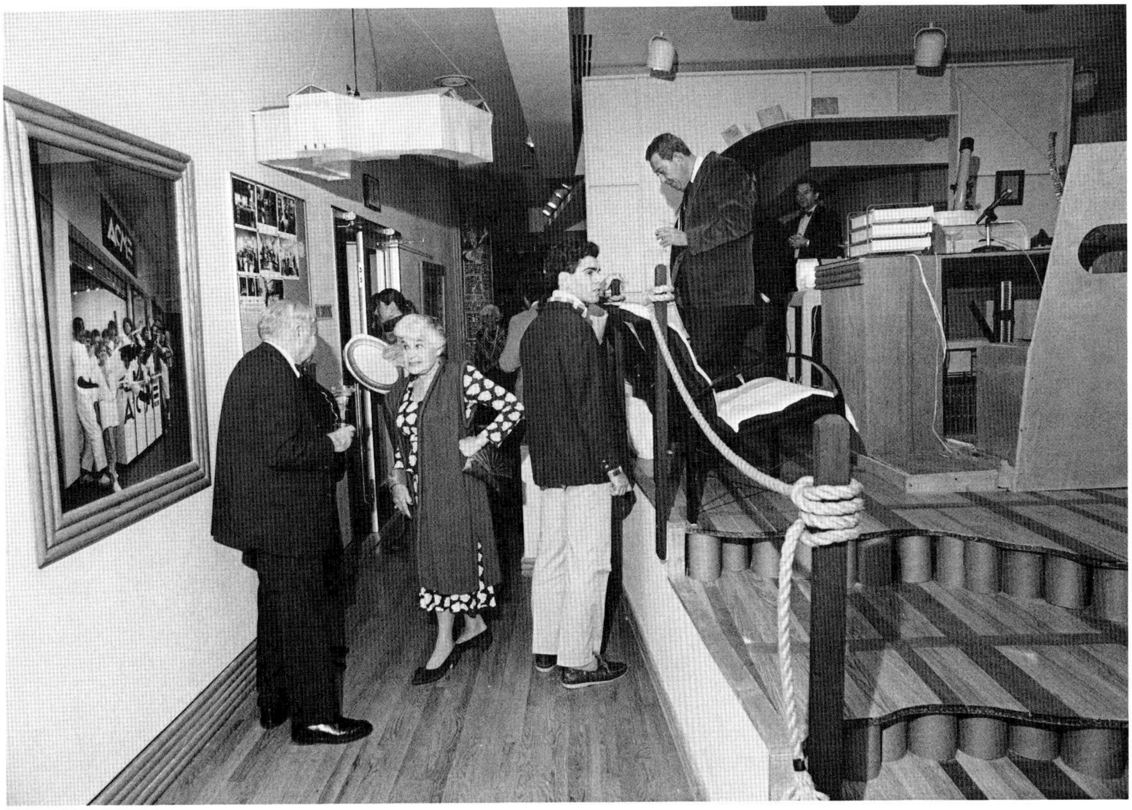

Opening night of DARING, showing American Enterprise Series documentation, Art Museum lamp, CEO Simkin's desk and stepped platform "office."

Simkin sees serendipity as "the glue that put [his] career together". But that is too simple an explanation of his working methods.

Simkin has created a truly public art, one that is inexorably connected to the fabric of life and one that invites participation from all sectors of society. In an age that can boast of no shared values and very few public institutions that truly serve the public, this is no small accomplishment.

Simkin's 'enterprises' often serve to blur the fuzzy boundary between art and life. This is the fifth in his **American Enterprise Series** which involve personal transactions in business situations. During the **DARING** installation several businessmen came into the Gallery to inquire about where they could buy the office furniture on display. One businessman asked if he could

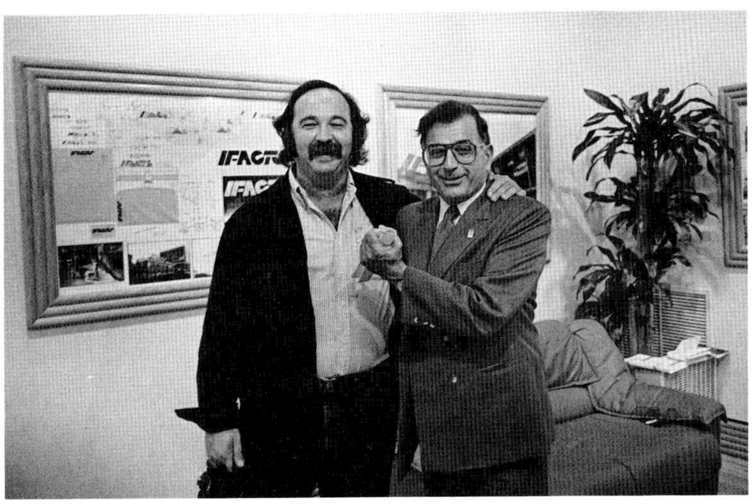

DARING President Phil Simkin jokes with Temple University President Peter J. Liacouras.

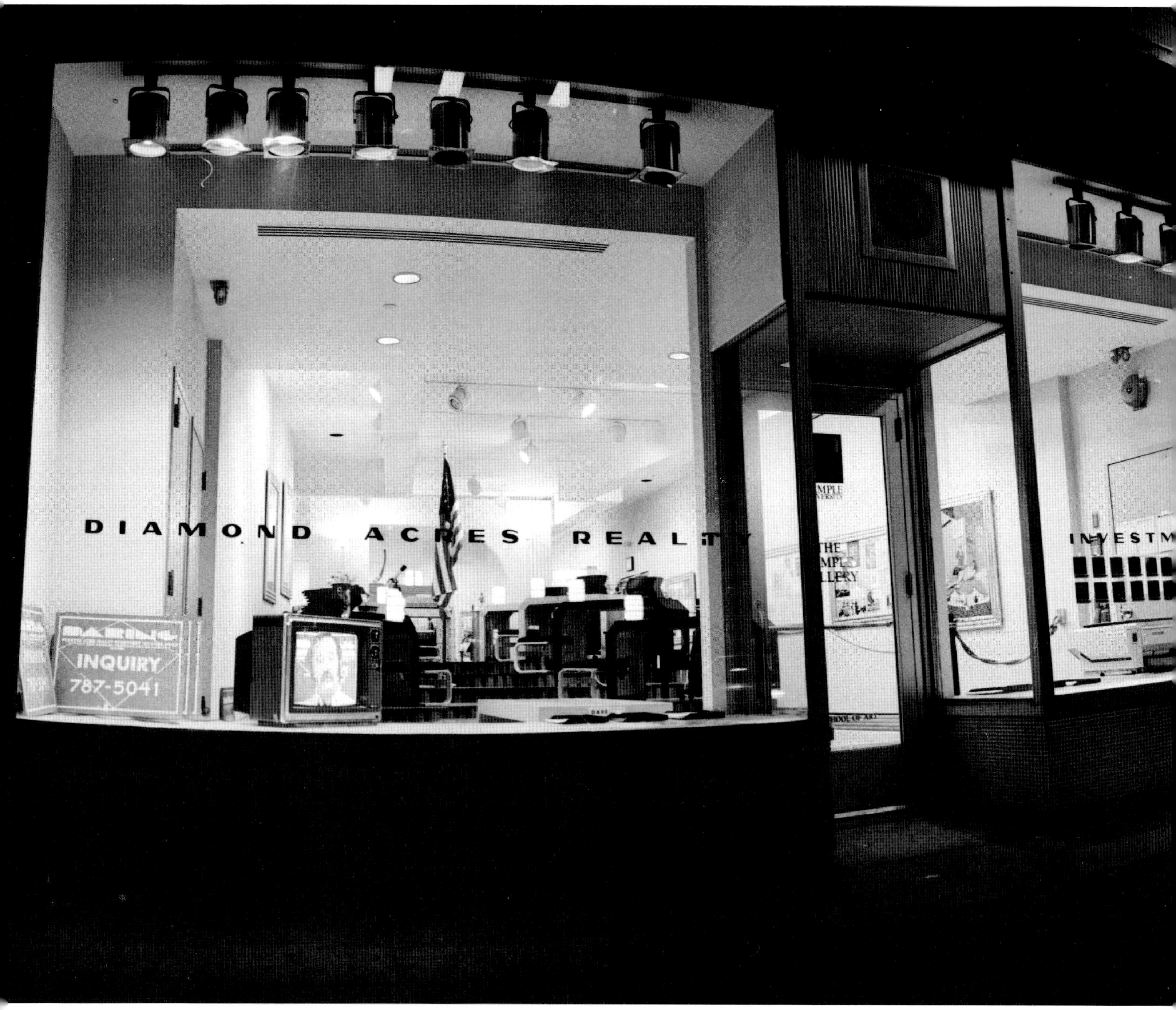

Evening view of DARING installation.

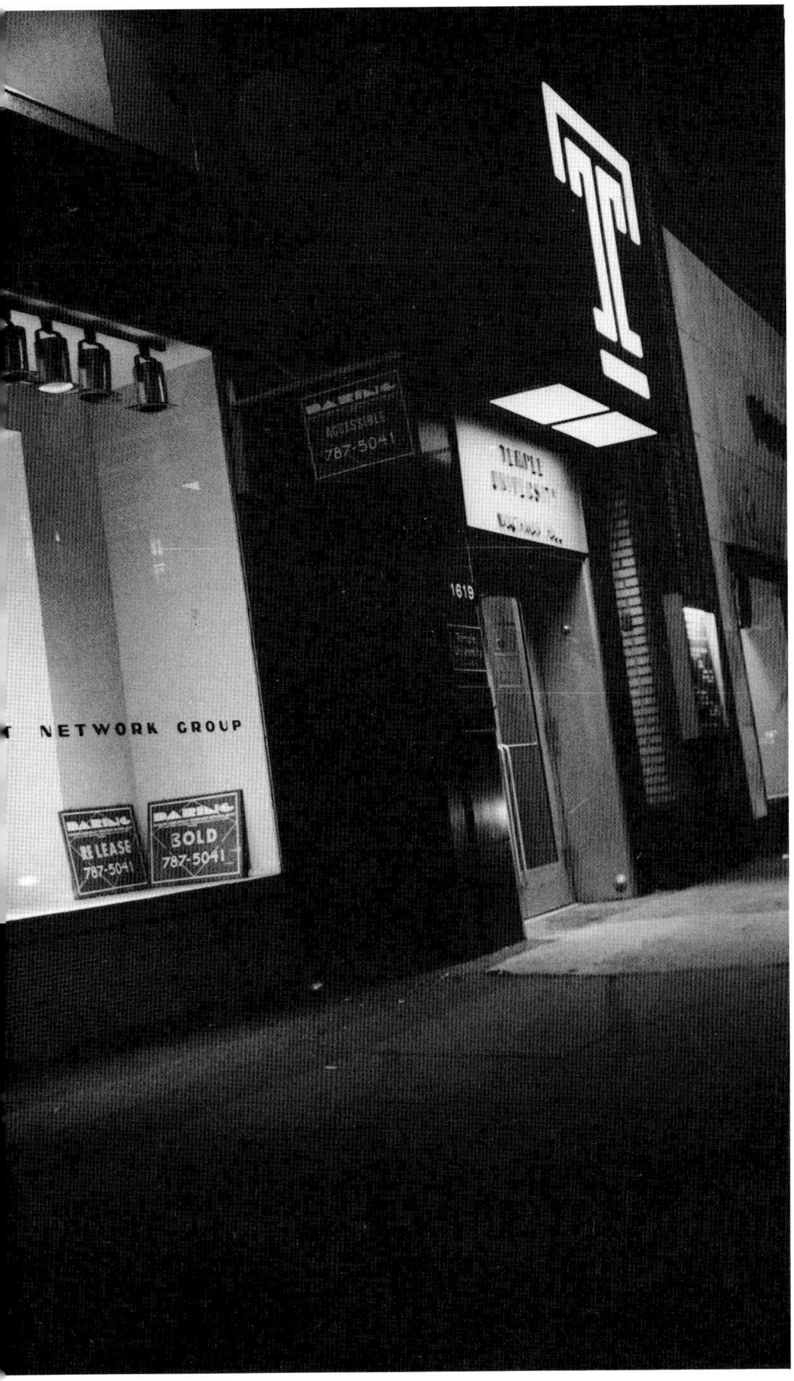

hold Chamber of Commerce meetings in the space. Visitors were intrigued; many were puzzled.

Simkin's installations require no advanced esthetic knowledge or judgment. They are meant to be ingratiating and inviting. The message the artist wished to convey with **DARING** was, "Come on in and see what we're about." The only problem was that once you were inside it was still not all that clear. The artist felt that his "... job was not to educate the viewer. They get out of it what they do."

After spending the better part of two days in the installation I decided that Simkin was right. The vistor had to pay attention and figure things out—much as one has to do in life. Many (if not most) life situations are not immediately clear or comprehensible.

Simkin's **DARING** installation was worth the effort it required. Both literally and figuratively it existed on many levels. Implicit, and perhaps most important, were the questions it raised about the role of both art and the artist in our society. Frequently it is said that today real estate and art are the only good and sure investments. Both are often pursued for greater gain and prestige. In **DARING** Simkin merged the art/real estate connection for more egalitarian ends—new opportunities for unknown artists, made possible without vast sums of money or years of planning.

Simkin has an almost unnerving ability to focus on issues of contemporary concern and illuminate them in an amusing and biting way. He begins with what is real and goes on to "invent, exaggerate, and extend." By appearing to make fun, Simkin makes us experience and see.

Artist: Lynn Denton
Property: 1623 South Street
(Rear lot facing Rodman Street)
Owner: Rob Solomon
Description: *Art is a Mark in the Dark* A performance by candlelight in which the artist wore a blindfold and a black and white costume to paint a mural on a prepared all-black surface using only white paint. The performer (Denton) "slowly transformed [the environment] from darkness to one in which white shapes formed a pattern illuminated by candlelight."

Artist: Anell Alexander
Property: 603 S. 10th Street
(Street-level window at 10th and South Streets)
Owner: Ray King
Description: In response to the multi-paned window, the artist constructed panels which listed the name of a person who had had a significant impact on her artwork, career and/or personal life within the year after she graduated with her MFA degree. The panels also contained a fabric swatch which came from her collection of garments, yardage, etc. with the idea that each swatch would "personify [her] perceptions of the person listed on each panel. The fabric sample might be similar to actual clothing that the person often wears, or it might represent a particular aspect of or feeling about the individual's personality."

Artist: Ann Reichlin
Property: Old shed and garden in Mt. Airy
Owner: Anne Greenberg
Description: The artist is working with the relationship of sculpture in conflict with domestic space. She will be thinking about the interior of the shed as a kind of "sanctuary in relation to the external forces of sculpture . . . and would like to change the context of the shed from something mundane to something that might possess some kind of secret." The materials used will be wood, wire, metal and paint.

Artists: John Riley Strockbine and Regina Kelly
Property: 15th and Mole
(Enclosed garden)
Owner: Neil Benson
Description: *Sights and Sounds of Philadelphia* Two or three musical compositions with a varying band will take place in the garden. "Improvisation will be directed toward a collective whole." Other original paintings and sculpture for the environment will be present. An abstract hand-made paper cityscape will be created for the small back wall which will take advantage of the available light.

Artist: Matthew Courtney
Property: 6441 Woodbine Ave.
(Two stone pillars with covered urns)
Owner: Don and Lynn Selkow
Description: Ideas include: insulation foam or plastic flowers overflowing and spilling down the sides of the pillars and onto the ground; or drawing all over everything with colored chalk.

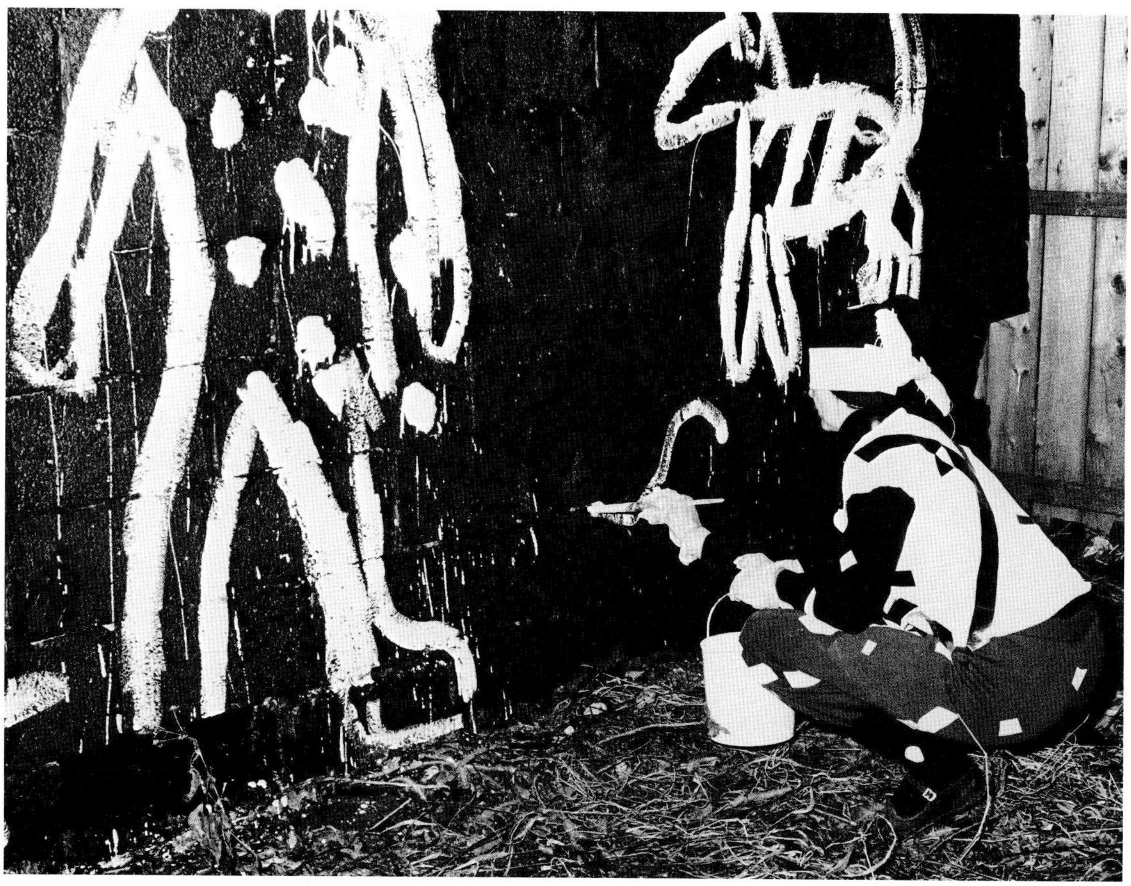

Lynn Denton during performance
Art is a Mark in the Dark.

Wide angle view and detail of Anell Alexander's *Graduation Window*.

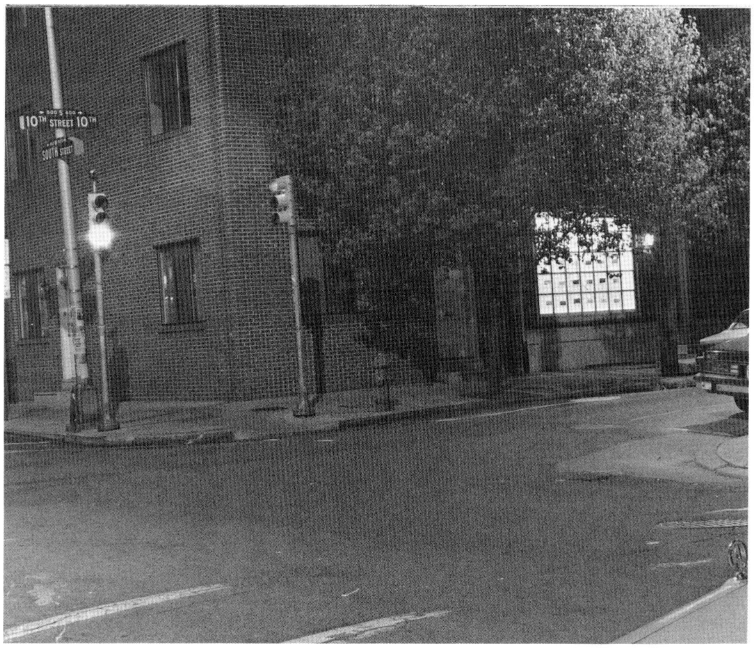

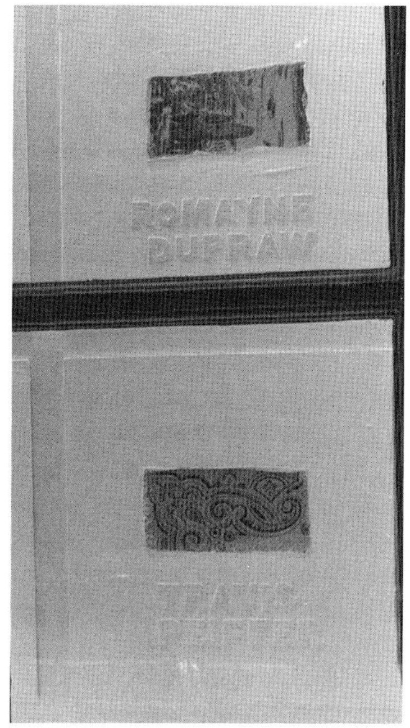

Artist: Margot de Wit
Property: Parking space wall on Van Pelt Street
Owner: Ed McGuire
Description: *Dichotomy #19*
Materials: plywood, tree trunks, and Astroturf. This piece will emphasize the "natural/unnatural and familiar/unfamiliar elements that have an inner coherence in harmony with both natural and man-made environments. Although the work shows harmony and balance in its composition, there is an incongruity between the different materials used. The Astroturf appears both to "intrude on the natural processes of growth (the living grass) and of disintigration (the dead tree), as well as being an integral part of those natural processes."

Artist: Carolyn Healy
Property: 1824 Delancey Place (Two large bushes in 5′ pots on sidewalk)
Owner: Ben Bernstein
Description: This piece was designed to be installed around election day and was to be "a symbolic depiction of George *Bush* lying about the CIA breaking the law in Nicaragua. Two wooden cartoon bubbles, one painted with red letters "CONTRAS?"; the other painted white with smoke stains and covered with screen would be placed above the bushes."

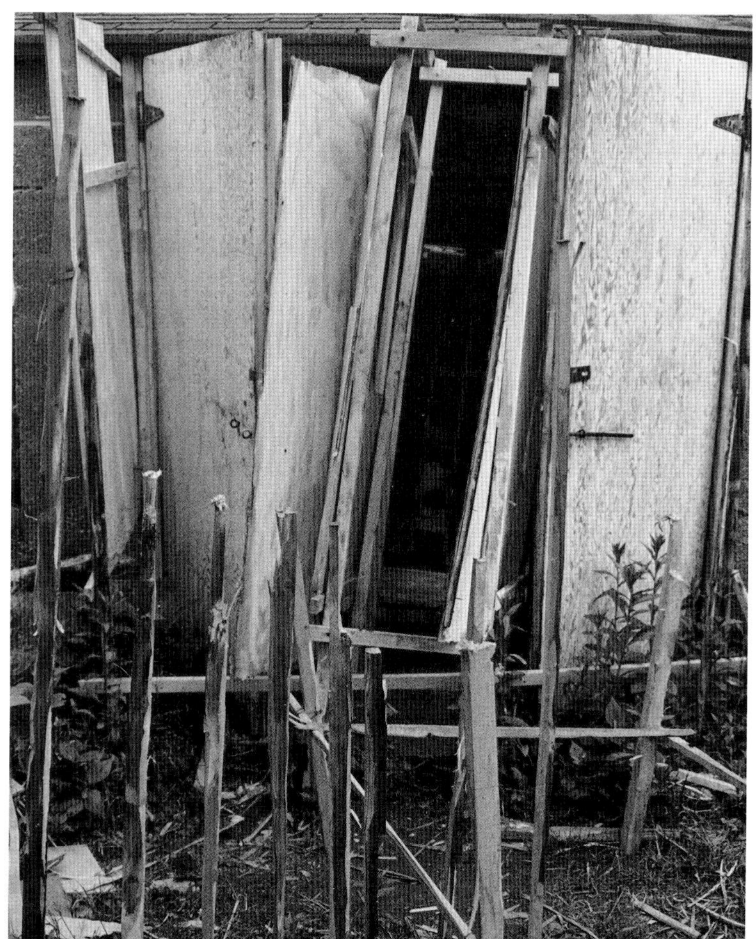

Sculpture by Ann Reichlin responding to interior space of shed.

Introduction and interview by Diane Karp, Twentieth Century Art historian and curator.

Phillips Simkin has been a fixture in the Philadelphia art scene since he graduated from Temple University, Tyler School of Art in 1965. He has, with his art, always managed to draw a broad spectrum of participation. His energy and wit have been evident in installations, happenings and events in locations as different as the Philadelphia Museum of Art and a luncheonette in the Italian Market. That is not to say that he works only in the City of Brotherly Love. His work has also been installed at ArtPark in Lewiston, New York, at the University of Maryland in College Park, Maryland, in North Dakota, San Francisco, California, Boston, and Lake Placid, New York.

Phillips Simkin is, as he so often says, a child of the Sixties. In art historical terms this description is a synonym for diversity. But the '60s diversity seems to imply a kind of awkwardness, a need to excuse itself from the main body of work that was generally held to represent the arts. The Sixties was clearly not the first period to create art that stood apart from the traditions and definitions of the discipline. The environments and happenings that have so influenced Simkin have a pedigree that can be traced into the early twentieth century. The Italian Futurists were perhaps the first to embrace the possibilities of EVENTS as art about man's displacement from order or as a method of focusing on issues beyond aesthetics and form. There were also the Russian Constructivist and Suprematist "total theater" ideas, as well as the outrageous theater associated with the Dada Theater Voltaire. In each case there was an implicit concern for the relationship between the arts and society and for the interaction of the audience in an experiential reassessment of their place in relation to both art and society. In the United States Allan Kaprow, Claes Oldenburg, Jim Dine and George Segal all believed that art should offer a new way to experience and see the world. With their happenings and installations, they strove not to create traditional enduring objects, but to offer a whole new view of art and life. Such experimental art that deviates from traditional expectation made the method or means of the event into a principal component of its meaning.

Not only the phenomenon of happenings but also minimal and conceptual art had a great deal of influence on Phil Simkin's work. His fascination with the pun and with other manipulations of language give yet another access route to viewer participation. The non-object art of the Sixties aspired to anti-formalist originality and a desire to make clear; socio-cultural criticism. All of these factors give us an insight into Phil Simkin, but ignore one absolutely vital element—humor. Perhaps the element that serves to distinguish Simkin's work is that Simkin's tongue is almost always planted firmly in his cheek. He pokes fun at the establishment, both social and artistic, and manages to draw the viewer in as participant in a non-threatening, enlightening engagement. Phil's temporary installations have about them the feel of Art Event As History: a history of detail and interaction, the ordinary brought into focus. His installations are often sculpture placed into a context that elicits participation as well as observation. What he manages with these installations is to turn them into real objects of human scale whose meaning arises from interaction. Although he always begins with an idea of how the piece will function, he sees himself as facilitator or perhaps *agent provocateur.* Phil's pieces always force us to look at ourselves as viewer, participant, neighbor, citizen and individual. Despite the humor and the element of entertainment, we usually depart from the interaction a bit wiser. He points to our strengths and weaknesses and allows us to reach our own conclusions—sort of like group therapy—and it feels good.

One of the central aspects of Phil Simkin's work is that it is temporary. It remains in place for an evening or a week or a month and then it is dematerialized—to be reborn only in drawings, diagrams or photographs, which hold only a fraction of the original. Participation cannot easily be documented and certainly cannot be experienced with any fidelity after the event. I propose to let the artist tell you about the ideas and issues behind his past works as well as his latest events—the **American Enterprise Series.**

Having feasted on a breakfast of fried eggplant sandwiches at the nearby culinary haven, Emil's, on Broad Street, Phil and I retreated to his second floor den to look at some slides and talk about art, life, and "anything that might fall into that crack in between."

PS O.K. Now we're not going back to pre-history, but we could go back to my training. I was a Tyler undergrad, and then went off to Cornell around 1965-67 for graduate school. In 1967-68 I had a post grad fellowship at the University of Pennsylvania and then I hung around Philadelphia for awhile teaching in the public school system through 1970.

I got my first full time teaching job at the University of Maryland in 1970. My career somehow correlates to those teaching postures because what I did in graduate school was really of little relevance, although it was all environments, installations—things which grew out of happenings and the whole Allan Kaprow influence and that kind of got its kick start at Cornell. All of my schooling saw me as a standard printmaker, painter-printmaker, even as Gene Feldman's post grad. printmaking fellow at Penn, I was always a printmaker with proclivities towards installation and environmental type things.

Here for example (pointing to a slide of a canary yellow tube) is an "inflatable." I stumbled into inflatables in graduate school and pursued it when I was at Penn because it was an economical means of enclosing a large volume of space—it was cheap, portable, could allow people to engage in the space from the inside as well as the outside, and it was easy to manage. This is a large yellow tube of lay flat polyethylene about four feet in diameter and it was set up on the campus of Union College in Schenectady, NY. I was invited up and I just simply unrolled a 200 foot tube of the stuff from one end of the knoll to the other with vacuum cleaners holding it erect and stones holding it down and it kind of looked pretty neat as this undulating yellow thing along the green campus. Then the trick was to get people inside of it.

DK Why yellow? Was that happenstance?

PS It was my choice, but there were not a lot of choices of poly tubing. They use it for liners for big sewer conduits and so you have black, green, clear and yellow. Yellow seemed to be reasonable and serendipitous because the sun coming through makes it even brighter, intensifying the color and the warmth of the experience. All of these experiences—I use the term 'experiential' which may be at this point a loaded word, but back then it seemed to rather aptly describe where I was coming from—were intended to set up experiential situations. And so, if one were to say, 'What kind of artist are you, Phil?' Well, I guess I'd say I'm an experientialist (if you can put an 'ist' on the end of it). I may not actually be that now, but it's still a nice catch-all word to describe me. My work has always had some participatory, engaged, interactive component. Human beings are part of it by the very nature of the idea behind each work. It's not objects that sit there passively for one to look at, they're usually structures or situations or environments or circumstances that allow me to set the moment in which other people . . . engage and '. . . do their thing.'

DK So when you speak of yourself as an 'experientialist,' you see yourself as the mediator between object/situation and the audience?

PS Oh yes, I am not a guru who is saying, 'Here is the piece, I speak great truth. Do this.' I am egocentric enough to feel that I have to be in charge and I have to design the event to achieve what I anticipate, but then I step aside and let the piece determine its own circumstance.

During the same period of time, 1970-71, I was also teaching a part-time class at Swarthmore College in the Art Department. It was a course on experimental art and it provided a chance to 'putz around' and do non-traditional things with a very unpredictable group of bright students. There was no such thing as an art major at Swarthmore, the kids just took all sorts of courses. It gave me the opportunity to do some odd things on campus and I was also invited to do an exhibition. My exhibition was a series of projects. One of these projects involved the 'blinding' of the Art and Music Building. I took paint, on which I had done some research and knew it would peel off, and I painted every window surface in the Fine Arts and Music Building. In effect I was psychologically blinding the building from the outside and restricting the enjoyment of the pastoral setting of the lovely Swarthmore campus from the inside. In other words there was no way to look out of or into this building—its eyes were closed.

DK Do you think this gesture was a bit aggressive for such a bucolic setting?

PS There were a number of issues functioning here. Swarthmore is quite 'Ivory Tower,' the students took their landscape for granted and so I addressed the seat of culture on campus in its symbolic role as repository of aesthetic knowledge. I wanted to create . . . a temporary restraint placed on that which had been taken for granted, (i.e., the eyes, the transparency of the windows of the building and its relationship to the campus and culture in general). Some interesting behavioral responses did occur. People began to scratch openings into the paint once they realized that the paint peeled away easily. This was usually on doors, but most people did not touch the painted windows, they simply sat in the rooms without any available contact with the outside.

DK Your sensibility of creating an environment or experiential setting is always one of temporarily transforming but never destroying the integrity of a given space. That makes your works . . . always fleeting. Is there something about them that makes them more intriguing to you because they don't have an ongoing lifespan and a monumentality about them?

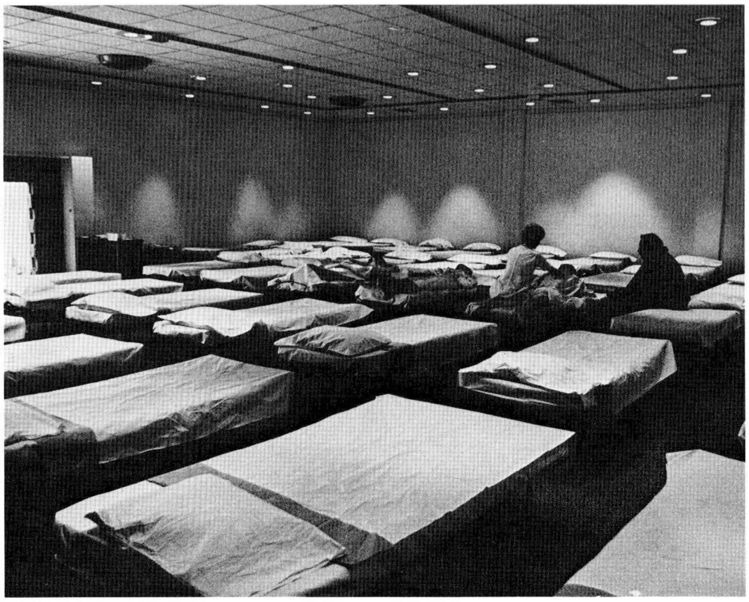

***Comfort Station, 1972,* University of Maryland Art Gallery, College Park, MD with beds, ICU nurse and relaxing participants.**

PS I'd say that has always been true and it still is true although it is perhaps now less so. Virtually all of my work has had a lifespan of one week, one month, maybe two months, but never longer than that. There is this dilemma that I am experiencing. As I grow older and as I do more work and as the basic memory of my work is these very slides that we are presently viewing, I realize that perhaps a longer lifespan is desirable. I have some doubts. Not that I want to start making concrete or welded steel monuments, but there has to be some middle ground where installation work can be temporary but perhaps less fleeting. I really don't know what the answer is.

DK Could part of the issue be the notion that people tend to grow numb to objects over long periods of exposure and they tend to react more willingly to new situations?

PS Yes, I think in general that is the case for public monuments and the like. Also, it is probably not an exaggeration to say that most public art is pretty tame. I would love to see some of my work have a longer span of existence but not necessarily be permanent.

1970-73 found me teaching at the University of Maryland and they offered me a major exhibition slot in the gallery. Like most institutions of this period, it was built of cinderblock walls, and I decided to cinderblock up the main doorway to the gallery and paint the blocks the same color as the walls around it, thus, making the gallery disappear for all intents and purposes. If you came to the gallery, there was a sign pointing to a solid cinderblock wall with floor molding, etc. A dead end.

For two weeks prior to the opening of the show during which time the gallery was 'nonexistent,' I placed a series of boxes along the wall with cards in them that identified some idea which would be addressed for a given date. They were all parodies of life at the University of Maryland's campus. Because every building on the campus had these fake wooden columns, one of the activity cards was a column counting card on which you were asked to count the columns all over campus and submit your estimate for a contest. We also had a carrot planting contest. It is a southern university, at least from my northern perspectives, and I figured that carrot patches were appropriate. I wrapped carrot seed strips around each card so that each person would take away the basic stuff to plant their own carrot patch. For every one of the days that the gallery didn't exist there was some specific University of Maryland activity card.

While all this was happening on the outside of the cinderblock wall I was on the inside of the gallery (to which I had access through a secret door) setting up a "comfort station," or basically an upgraded massage parlor. I borrowed a bunch of folding hospital beds and paper sheets and pillowcases. We built changing rooms each with a light and mirror and curtain. One of my graduate students was an intensive care nurse, so I got her into this. On the appropriate day we sledgehammered through the cinderblock wall we had placed in the gallery entrance to make it visible. Now everybody could once again enter the gallery and we could begin phase two of the project, which was the re-definition of the University of Maryland Art Gallery as a Comfort Station. Visitors would come into a darkened space where an attendant was seated at a desk by the front door. She would try to make you comfortable. You could go into a changing booth, remove your clothing, don a hospital gown and then take a nap during the hot summer day. If you wanted, the attendant would give you a cooling alcohol back rub or massage.

DK Were you aiming at the Matissian idea of art being like the comfort of an easy chair?

PS I didn't have that in mind although I basically agree. Most of my work does not evolve from art historical references although the philosophy of Matisse suits the goals of the work.

It was also meant to address that particular place, that particular time, that particular environment and those particular people. It was a rather outrageous gesture: turning a University campus art gallery into a proto-pleasure palace. Not pleasure in the sexual context, but pleasure in the feeling relaxed and comfortable sense. It is not outrageous that a person would want to escape the heat and the din of a southern summer day and the campus book 'larnin' just to unwind.

DK So the people became the objects as well as the audience?

PS Those who came into the gallery and chose to take their clothes off—remember this was the early Seventies and young people took their clothes off all the time—under a controlled situation inside the institution [served] to knock many barriers down. To lie there in little more than a hospital gown and allow yourself to be tended to is a total reversal of the normal, staid expectations of a university art gallery experience, especially at Maryland.

DK Here you managed to have your audience submit as well as actively participate. They are both viewer and performer. The activity of breaking through with sledgehammers, was that meant to be irreverent?

PS To be sure . . . Tearing down a wall in an institution with sledgehammers is a fairly violent and brutal, dirty, messy activity, and when it is done it usually involves construction, not destruction, and what's more it is usually accomplished by construction people. Here we had art people knocking down the walls of the temple to reach the inner sanctum which had been redefined by the artist. There are lots of not-so-obscure symbolic references here.

DK Your concern for symbolic references and the transformation of normal expectations for art has been central from the very early years of your work.

PS Another early use of these principles was **The Public Center for the Collection and Dissemination of Secrets.** This was sponsored by the Institute of Contemporary Art, at the University of Pennsylvania, as part of the first "Made in Philadelphia" show. This was part of what Director Suzanne Delahanty called an 'urban sites exhibition.' The five artists involved in the "Made in Philadelphia" show did pieces in various locations in the city. With Suzanne's help I got the cooperation of Bell Telephone who set up all these temporary phone positions at 30th Street Amtrak Station. The help of a young fellow, Peter Voetsch, who was the resident genius, was enlisted to figure out how to make all the whiz-bang electronic circuitry work. Remember, this was 1973, which was the time of the Watergate bugging era. I decided to allow a situation in which everyone could bare their breast and expose any of their secrets or private bits of information, selected items that they wished to share with an anonymous public. This was a basic recording system which was designed to be familiar equipment. You simply entered any one in a bank of perfectly ordinary looking phone booths, picked up the receiver, pushed a button and told a secret. As with almost all things in life you have to give to get, so after telling your secret you would get a reward: you could then push another button and get to hear someone else's secret. The system was designed with a continuous loop of tape that I would recharge with all new recorded secrets every night at about midnight. I could thus edit out the potentially slanderous stuff and keep it lively. This was truly a public utility and I think I was probably the

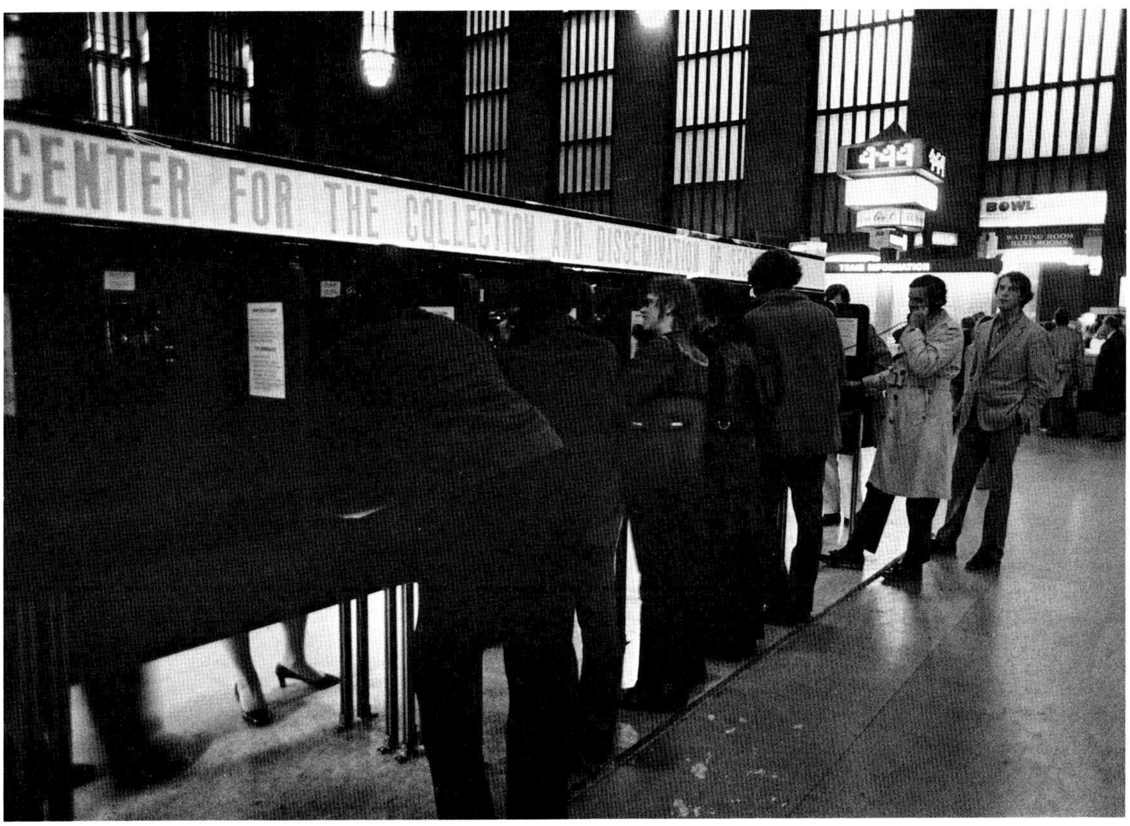

Public Center for the Collection and Dissemination of Secrets, **30th Street Amtrak Station, 1973 Urban Sites phase, Made In Philadelphia I, Institute of Contemporary Art, University of Pennsylvania. Panelescent sign overhead with 20 telephones and relay system, master tape recorder and slave units to permit the public exchange of private secrets, 24 hours a day for three weeks.**

***Your Fifteen Minutes,* 1973, Made In Philadelphia I, Institute of Contemporary Art, University of Pennsylvania.**

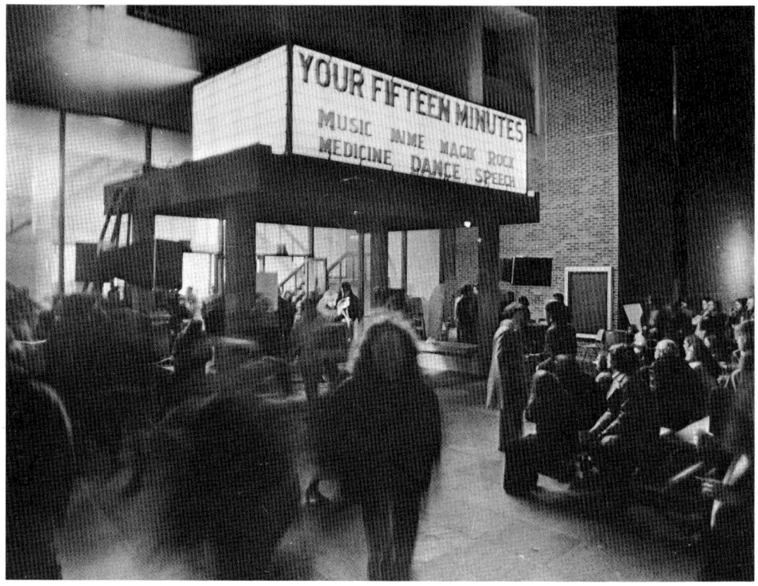

first, or at least one of the first artists to do this kind of installation.

DK Like the piece you did at Maryland, each participant is audience and performer, confessor and confessee, voyeur and exhibitionist.

PS Yes, I tried to keep everything familiar and ordinary on the surface. The only thing I added was the luminescent panel at the top which read **Public Center for the Collection and Dissemination of Secrets,** and that was made by me as a customized touch that for all intents and purposes appeared to be an ordinary bank of telephones. So there it sat, glowing in the dark like a beacon waiting for you to come over and tell your secrets.

DK What makes this piece even more unassuming is that it is the nature of ordinary banks of telephones that as private as they might appear you always hear what the person next to you is saying. In fact, a part of being at such a public telephone is being able to communicate and eavesdrop at the same time. To me you joined two activities that are a natural.

PS As well as the implied humor in light of the national focus on Watergate. That was a prime issue for me. It was going on as a matter of public policy by our President. Why not bring it down to the level where ANYBODY could indulge in the same gamesmanship.

DK That is why I found it so funny that the article on this piece was printed on the same page of the newspaper as an article about G. Gordon Liddy.

PS Yes, it was Watergate and **Secret Center** and it made the national news—it went out on AP.

At the same time that the **Secret Center** was installed in 30th Street Station, I also did two other pieces at the ICA for the "Made in Philadelphia" exhibition. I did a parody on the Warhol comment that someday everybody would be famous for 15 minutes. So I got the marquee from the old World Theater which was being torn down at 19th & Market, and I got some bleachers from the Physical Education Department at Penn, and other equipment needed for setting up a continuous performance arena. We would put your name 'up in lights' if you called in before hand to reserve a time slot to perform in, or you could just come along and take over if there was no one else performing. It ran 24 hours per day, the lights on the marquee went on automatically, two spotlights focused on an always live microphone, there was outdoor carpeting on the ground to distinguish the area at the entry to the ICA as a special performance zone. Anyone could climb onto the bleachers and just hang out or listen to the performances.

***Displacement Project II,* Philadelphia Art Museum 1974. View of West Foyer installation of 20,000 cardboard pinhole cameras.**

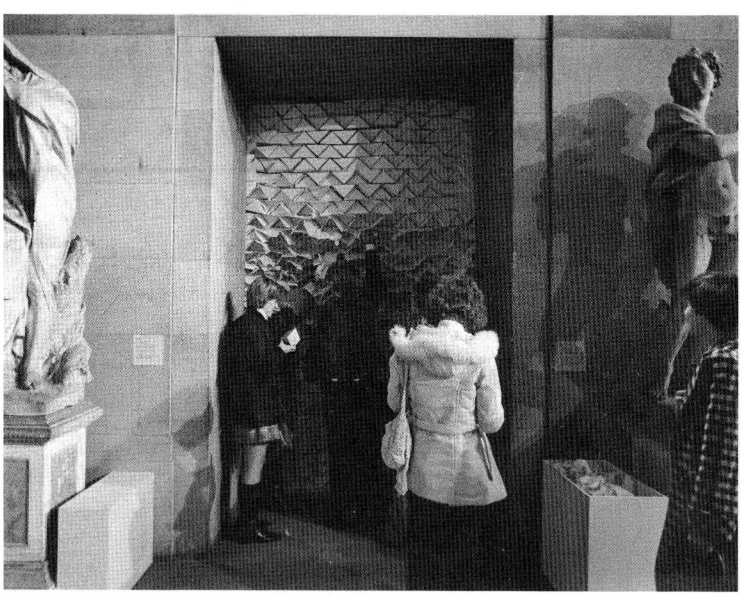

This was the first legitimate exhibition opportunity that I had, and it is to the credit of Director Suzanne Delahanty and the ICA that I had a chance to do an inside piece, an outside piece and an outreach piece. I look upon this as the beginning of my professional career as an artist.

DK Each of the pieces was deeply concerned with process and participation as well as a subtle nod to politics. Sort of like the three "P"s of Phil Simkin: participation, process and politics.

PS In 1973, with a small NEA grant I did a piece at the ICA in Boston which also involved the three "P"s. **Displacement Project** was a piece where we hand-assembled pinhole cameras which were loaded into a tractor trailer which was then driven around to various parts of Boston where it would sit and invite the public to remove a cardboard pinhole camera from the solid packed mass of the trailer.

A year later I was invited by Penny Bach to do a similar project for the Community Programs Department of the Philadelphia Museum of Art. It happened at that moment in time when the PMA was getting ready to close in order to install air conditioning. This was sort of an invitation to the community to come in and have fun and say goodbye to the Museum for about a year. Perhaps that is one of the reasons they allowed something as participatory and unusual as this piece.

I selected the doorway to the West Foyer because it was a self contained room. We hand-manufactured the cameras in the Museum and stacked them in the doorway according to a system I devised with self-stick paper (sort of like a bricks and mortar situation) and we carefully set it up so that each camera could be removed from the 'wall' by pulling it forward. I called this work **Displacement Project** because you literally displaced physical space from a self-contained volume of an architectural entity in order to take this one-shot camera home and displace pictorial space.

The cameras were beautiful. I worked with Container Corporation of America and between their designer and my ideas and modifications we came up with a remarkable triangular camera complete with the "Simkin flap" which made it light proof. Actually it won a design award for CCA in the competition for packaging design that year.

The Museum then built a public darkroom so that after a person took a camera and exposed the film inside they could return to the Museum, using the camera to gain admission, and assistants in the darkroom would help them process their picture. If it was a dud, they would load it up with fresh film and they would try again. If it was a good shot they could see the positive right there, take one copy home with them and we would put one copy on display.

DK In an elegant way the **Displacement Project** dealt not only with the displacement of pictorial space and the displacement of the physical space of each camera, but also with the displacement of the doorway by the wall of cameras and the imminent displacement of the Museum. Also there was the displacement of high art by ordinary people's art.

PS Ah yes, and that brings us to the project done in the summer of 1975 at ArtPark: **Commodity Exchange-Par Value.** This was part of the Artist-in-Residence program, a program which invited artists to do site specific installations. I pre-constructed 50 boxes at an electrical metal box manufacturer in Philadelphia. I wanted 2′ × 2′ × 2′ metal boxes with handles and hinged lids which printmaker Lois Johnson helped me etch with the appropriate words using nitric acid. Then each metal lid was inked and wiped and then zinc coated to protect it. Like the printmaker that I am deep inside there was the desire to make a fine object in multiples.

During '75–76, using funding from an NEA grant, I built the piece which I was to use at ArtPark in the summer of 1976 as a special event, in effect. This was the first public installation of my maze, **Choices-Prototype.** The maze consisted of a complicated system of swinging doors with a word system which I devised with the help of a writer and a sociologist. It was designed to be modular, portable, easily assembled, and to fit into two 24′ U-Haul trucks. The premise was that you zig and zag through the maze either randomly or by a sequence of choices relating to the words painted on each of the hollow core swinging doors. These binary choices were set up in such a way that the choice to the left would be liberal, the choice to the right, conservative; the choice to the left American Indian, the choice to the right Colonialist; to the left Libertarian, to the right cautious, etc.

They were all American referenced word pairs. Some were simply numerical. Once you were in the maze there was no concern about getting lost. It was more an issue of pathways and patterns of movement. Where you exited the maze was determined by the pathway resulting from your choices in each cubicle. There were seven possible places to exit the maze and we gave out buttons which designated the specific exit. The button served as a symbol of how each person exited the maze.

The piece had its second life at P.S. 1 in Long Island City, NY where I was invited to install the maze in the school yard during the fall of 1976. There it had an interesting life because during the weekends the neighborhood kids would use it as a clubhouse by covering over the central portion with plywood. During the week people would come out to go through it in the normal fashion.

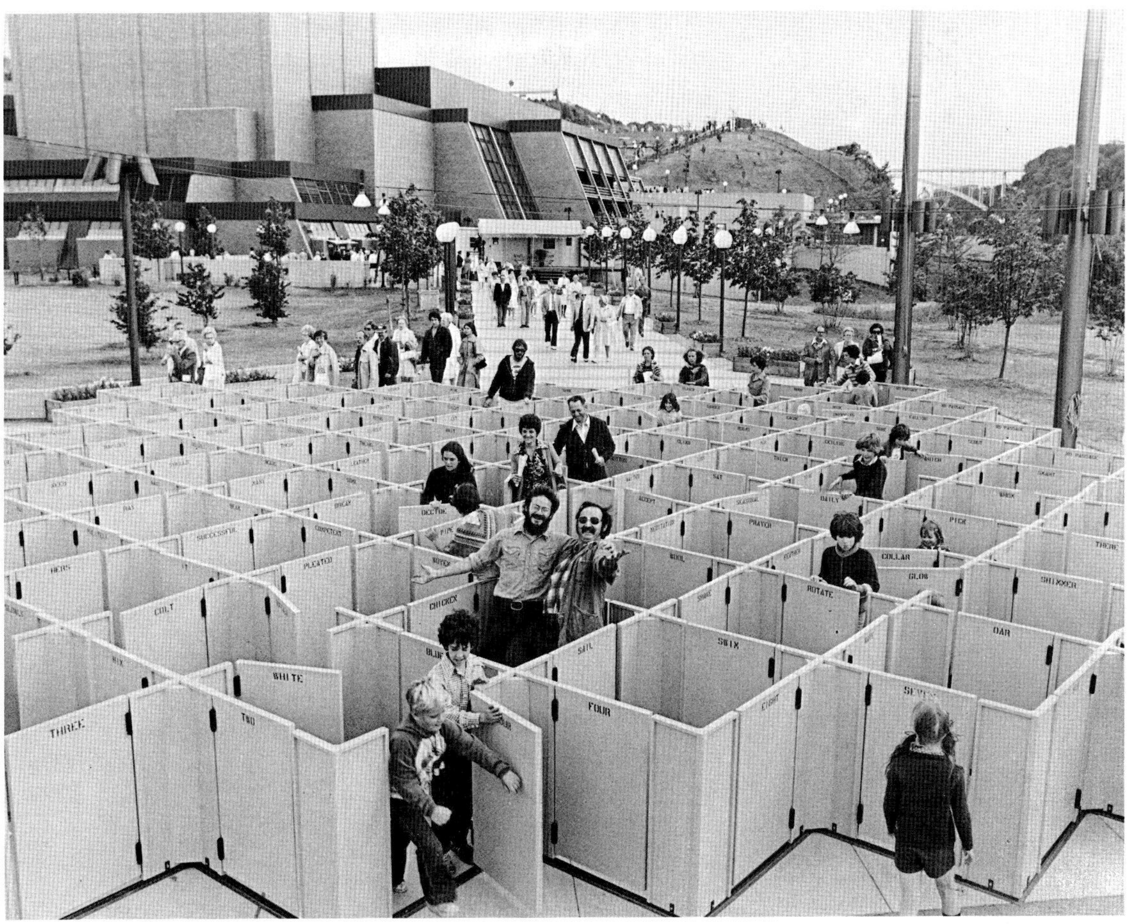

***Choices Maze*, ArtPark 1976, Lewiston, NY. View of *Choices* decision-making maze installed on theater plaza.**

The third life was part of the Bicentennial in Philadelphia in November 1976 through January of 1977. It was set up on J.F.K. Plaza.

DK For a temporary installation this piece had a rather long life span. Did this affect your choice of materials?

PS The fabricator built it well and it could have been permanently installed with little change, but it was always meant to be temporary.

DK This piece underscores your idea of setting up a situation but not maintaining control.

PS I have never been interested in asserting control. I am interested in implying control by the nature of the structure I set up.

DK You always assert the fact that you are not concerned with the overriding aesthetics of these works, yet they are usually very handsome objects visually, and they tend to have a great deal of aesthetic content.

Most often the underlying form is a grid but even when that is not the case there is the implicit concept of a single shape which is multiplied. It appears often as though it could be infinitely expanded either by extension or by use.

PS The objects which I create must be used and in that way expanded; otherwise they are lifeless. I guess, for me, the objects are means to an end. They are designed for participation and are not complete without such actual or at least potential use.

I have always favored the geometric, architectural options in sculpture. The modular or grid system is to my mind supremely functional and useful because of the internal logic of stability.

I think of myself as a problem solver. Each new situation provides a new problem, I need to rethink and analyze each situation. Another example of situation specific problem solving to foster participation and communication was the project I did at ArtPark in 1975. This was my **Human Puzzle,** which was a 40′ diameter foam rubber puzzle made of 76 pieces which were worn about the waist of each of 76 participants. The players had to wander about and decide where they fit.

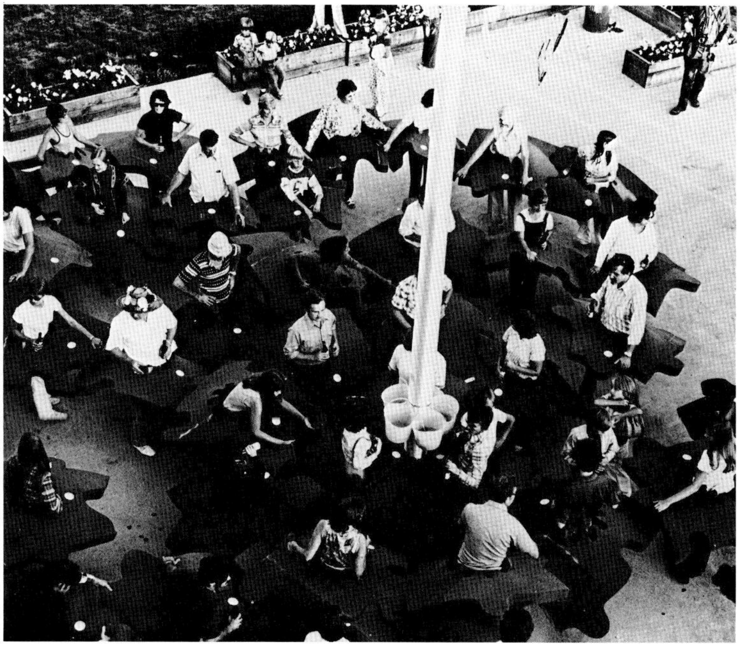

***Human Puzzle, 1975,* ArtPark, Lewiston, NY. Overhead view of 76 piece foam jigsaw puzzle being worn and put together under artist's direction.**

DK It is a metaphor for society—the game of life.

PS On one level it is a silly child's game suitable for the "Price Is Right," but on another level it is about the sociology of the way people get along together when there is a mutual gain and they are dependent upon complete strangers for success. You are forced to talk and interact, to form groups and basically work together.

DK And where was Phillips Simkin in all of this?

PS This piece only works if I am there with my megaphone huckstering. I provide the overview of the event and provide encouragement. I guess I'm sort of a friend of the court or implementor. In this piece I play a performance role and act as facilitator because it could not happen by itself.

DK You have managed again, within an entirely new situation, to elicit opposing emotions or activities. You have set up an environment where a pattern of action and movement has been pre-determined and yet always leaves options for investigation open. You almost ask the viewer to go against his better judgment in order to achieve the effect.

PS I want to challenge the audience but I have no interest in being authoritarian. I set the scene and leave the utilization to the viewer. Once it begins I don't like to meddle so that the participant becomes the driving force, the energy that makes the piece whole.

In 1979, I was invited to have an exhibition at the Pennsylvania Academy of Fine Arts, in the Morris Gallery. The Academy is hallowed in the history of American art; it is precious and austere and required a special project to address its special status. What I created was a stage set which addressed the division in society between the "haves" and "have-nots." I divided the Morris Gallery in half and built a door as entry to each of the two parts. One door was very tall and served as the door of the privileged, while the other was low and square and served the less privileged. Dividing the two spaces was a canvas wall which was replicated in the "haves" and "have-nots" space. Both sides of the canvas wall were gridded, and on the grid was a rebus, a riddle game to discover where I had hidden the key to the Pennsylvania Academy of Fine Arts. The key was hidden somewhere in Philadelphia and there were two parts to this city game. First you had to figure out the rebus riddle which would provide you with a clue to where the key was hidden. Then you had to find the key and you would be rewarded with the world's most precious object, which was my excuse for going to the Liberty Bell to take a direct casting of the crack. From that negative void which constitutes the crack, we took a direct casting which created a positive volume that the world had never seen before. The crack which symbolizes so much to so many was now transformed from negative space to positive volume.

The rebus riddle went like this:

Near other cracks artistically rare
We sit upon the bench and stare
Beholding a marriage of ironic debris
Between your legs lies the key

In order to solve the rebus the audience first had to construct the rebus on the canvas wall in each of the two gallery spaces at the PAFA. This was done by pulling a square of fabric from a gum ball jar and then matching it by its number to the like numbered square and pinning it in place. Once enough of the rebus was in place two folks did indeed find the key.

DK Where?

PS Well, you're an Art Historian, let's test your skill.

DK The Arensberg Collection? The bench in front of the "Large Glass?"

PS It was taped under the bench in front of Duchamp's "The Bride Stripped Bare by Her Bachelors, Even" known as the "Large Glass." The two people who figured it out found the key under the bench, jumped up, tried to explain the whole thing to the guards, etc. A real scene. The crack was then donated to the PAFA in the name of the finders, and it stayed in the archives in the basement of the Academy. When it became clear that the crack was not going to be accepted into the permanent collection I took it back. The crack will serve as a continuing theme in my work so it doesn't end here.

One of my few non-participatory pieces was created as my part of the summer Artist-in-Residence program at the Brooklyn Museum of Art. It was an installation of indoor tile which I laid by hand outdoors on the grounds of the Brooklyn Museum, near the botanical gardens. I decided to create a simple deteriorating surface using indoor tile because I knew full well that with the cycles of seasons it would expand and contract and become sort of like a Roman ruin. I used textured and smooth white tiles to work out the question, **'Is there anything else you want to tell me?'** It was only effectively visible from above, either the upper floors of the museum or from heaven. It is an enigmatic question because it seems there is no proper answer; there is never anything else you want to tell someone, yet there is always something else you want to say.

DK There seems to be a more personally reflective quality to this piece. You have made a less temporary installation which ages and records the passage of time yet remains fixed to its location. You also pointed out that to really see it you must view it from above so, who is the audience—besides Phil Simkin?

PS I guess this is my commemorative piece for my father who had passed away some time before. That was a question I had heard many times in my childhood, "Phillips, is there anything else you want to tell me?" There always was and never was, I wasn't going to tell him that I dented the fender or spilled the ink on the carpet, but he always asked. It is a phrase loaded with meaning for me and is certainly, in this context, a personal reflection on my father and my relationship with him. The nice thing for me is that the piece may still sit behind the Brooklyn Museum and no one would ever know that it is an installation because all the tiles have broken and popped and so you can't really see the letters or read the message. It was an installation which was meant to have an aging and passing process; ashes to ashes. Vestiges remain of the piece, yet it passes as an object.

DK It is a metaphor for your relationship to your father in that the person passes but the vestiges remain?

PS The same is true for a work of art. Is it necessary for the work to be present in order to make an impact? Nothing is forever or permanent. I guess I made an anti-monument monument in a personal way.

To a Fault . . . 1978, Morris Gallery exhibition project, Pennsylvania Academy of the Fine Arts. Installation view of rebus riddle game at left, the "Historic Break" (Liberty Bell crack) prize at right.

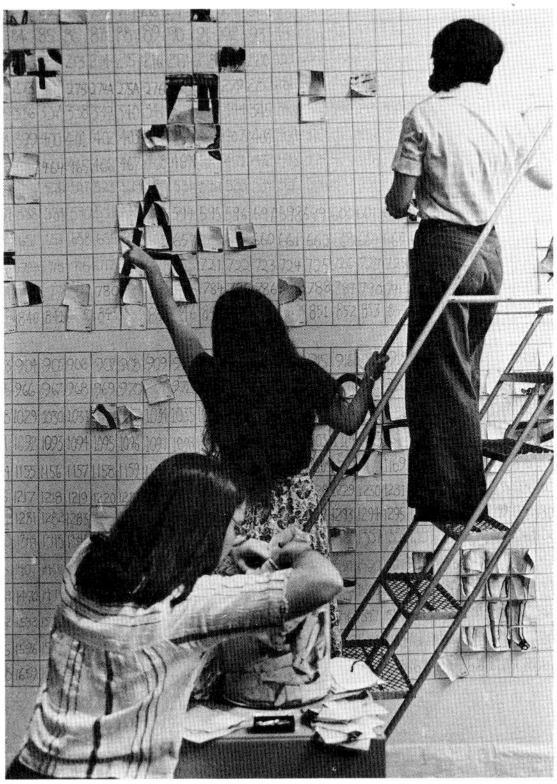

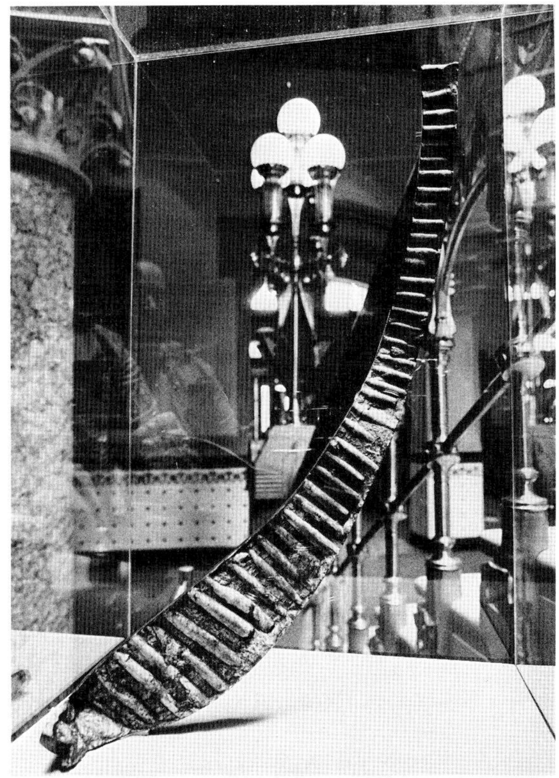

In 1980 I was invited to create a work of art for the Winter Olympics in Lake Placid. What I did was to build an ark on sleds which I called **ROSEBUD II.** I proposed to build seven self-propelled earthly parodies which would be mobile via sleds so it could then move across frozen Mirror Lake. The project was 180 feet long by 30 feet tall by 15 feet wide. Each house had a tall mast at the center designed so that the aluminum frame structure of the houses could be raised on the mast like the curtain on a proscenium stage or a sail on a boat. Each house was sheathed in quilted rip-stop nylon which had been stuffed with duck feathers which we blew into the material in a church in Germantown before the Olympics. It is the most ambitious project to date and was still temporary despite the scale of the piece physically and as well as the labor involved. It took us two weeks to set up in Lake Placid and the Olympics only lasted 13 days.

DK It is the nature of such 'polar' existence that it is temporary because the lake eventually thaws and the solid surface on which you have built it is no longer solid.

PS It was an extreme life situation. We lived with the cold and snow and tourists. It was not easy art to make. Each house was a parody on one of the stages of life from Willy the Shakes' *As You Like It,* from infancy to senility. The trappings in each of the houses related to the particular stage of life.

DK But within the context of the Olympic community they served other purposes?

PS Oh yes, they served as shelters and as magnets. There was an electric propane generator to provide warmth. We were like a beacon of warmth glowing out on the frozen lake.

DK What kind of trappings did you put into the houses?

PS Well, for an example, the middle house, which was 'the young soldier winning at any cost,' was supplied with seven pinball machines which I customized white on white. The athletes and tourists and newsboys and diplomats all came out to the ark and played for free to reach the highest score.

DK Did you play an active role there or was it more as observer?

PS That's funny because I was one of the only artists who came up to the Olympics with the art. Most people had built the work the year before and sent the work up to sit there waiting for the snow to fall. That would have made no sense for me because being there and being part of the event was so important. I was part of the **ROSEBUD II** crew.

In 1982, because I was an adjunct part-timer on the faculty at Moore College of Art I was asked to come up with an idea to mark the inauguration of the fourth President of Moore. I couldn't resist doing something totally reasonable and absurd at the same time, and so we 'elevated' Edward McGuire in full academic regalia to his new position. The carpenter built a gangplank which extended straight out from the building floor above. We laced flat polyethylene tubing in a huge 'V' to inflate with air and mark the opening. After the induction ceremony in the library, the procession led out to the sidewalk from which McGuire ascended to the Presidency and penetrated the building high above the crowd below.

DK You use the word 'penetrate' which in this case seems a bit loaded with references. Moore is a women's college of art and the President ascended or rose and then penetrated the school.

PS Remember, I am a site-specific artist. I solve the problem according to the situation, the environment, the participants and the idea that relates to a specific situation. This male President entered through the fourth floor window because he was the fourth President, so you see it all had meaning and allusion.

Site-specificity is also in the eye of the beholder. For instance in 1982 I did a one week piece at the University of North Dakota. The University, in Grand Forks, is near a Strategic Air Command base, or SAC. So I built a catapult in the

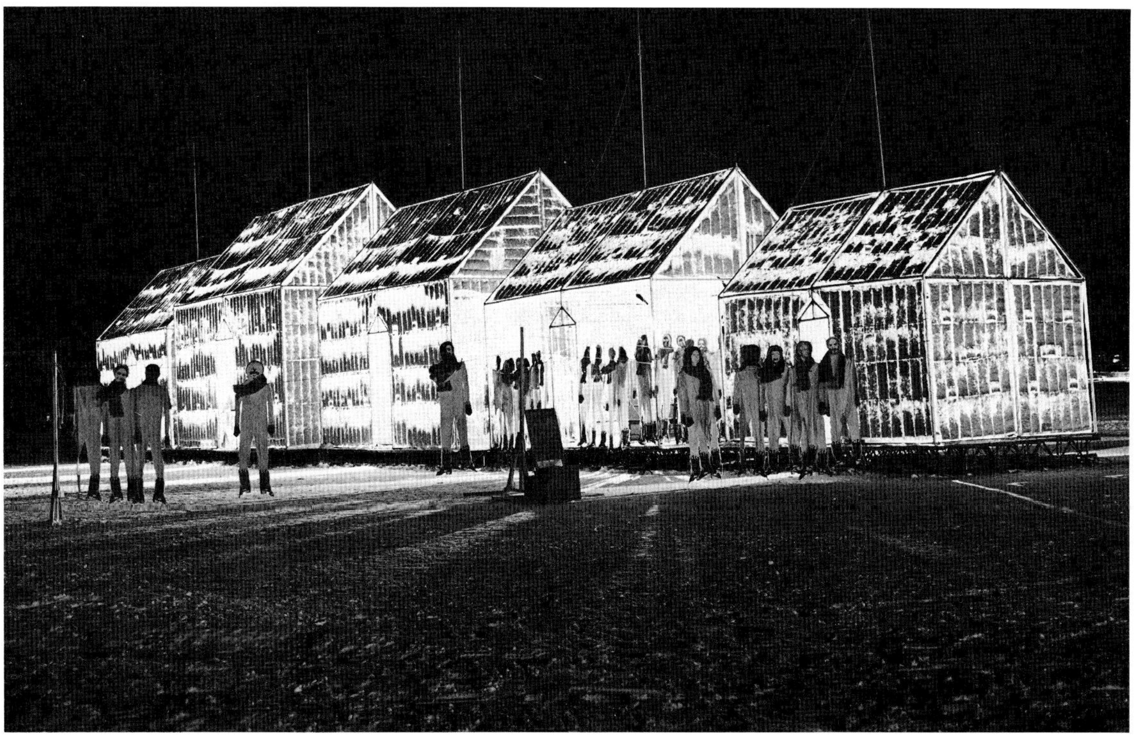

***Rosebud II—Seven Self-Propelled Earthly Parodies,* XIII Winter Olympics, Lake Placid, NY, 1980. Night view on frozen Mirror Lake of 180′ long ark attended to by *Audience Frieze* by Lois Johnson.**

campus shop and called this piece **SAC IT TO 'EM.** The piece was designed so that your body weight acted as the counter force to work the catapult. We rolled out words in the snow using a rubber roller which had been cast in Philadelphia and then applied red and green food coloring to the words (red and green are the University's colors). We then scooped up the tinted snow words, placed them in the catapult basket and hurled them across the frozen river. Trajectories, who can make their words go farthest, using your weight, throwing your words, this all added up to my attempt at an armaments piece where one hurls words rather than missiles.

Here is a case where my Liberty Bell crack found another existence. In 1983 I was invited to submit a proposal for a monumental piece of sculpture to be sited between the new SmithKline Beckman building and the Franklin Plaza. Anyway, it was eventually selected as the sculpture project that would be recommended to the Board. This model won the battle and lost the war.

Between 1980 and 1984 there were no major projects. I live for moments which I cannot invent, I must wait for those moments to find me. I did a series of quickies like the North Dakota and Moore pieces, but nothing particularly major occurred for a while.

DK How did the first project in your **American Enterprise Series** come about?

PS In 1984 I was invited to submit a proposal for the Capp Street Project in San Francisco. This was a house designed to be an architectural structure in which artists would come and do projects without physically altering the building. You could change things or change the way the house was used, but the basic structure had to be maintained. While you were Artist-in-Residence, you had a nice living space on the second floor of the house. I spent a great deal of time thinking about the area and the time and since the Democratic convention was taking place, the Summer Olympics were coming up at the end of that summer, Silicon Valley was there and there was this Eastern kid going West, I decided that what was necessary was **Cable Knitted News.** At this point I was beginning an **American Enterprise** cycle of commenting on and role playing about American industry and entrepreneurship. **CKN** was my answer to a media event and I felt that for the time and place it was the right answer.

I invented my own corporate conglomerate. I was sure that I wanted it to be a news operation but a newspaper was too mundane, as were newsletters and radio stations, so I started to think about computers and knitting and stitches and jacquard and (of course) grid systems. I learned that there are computerized knitting systems. I convinced a knitting machine company, Stoll America, to lend me a machine and also to transport it out to California. Anyway they did indeed send me a computerized machine and a British technician to make it do my bidding. A single thread of white and a single thread of black knitted the entire 'page' of news. I set up the gallery as though it was a young contemporary corporate entity which suits the high tech nature of the house. We looked venture capital all the way. I had designed a logo which was woven into patches to identify those who represented **CKN** and we used the logo on the company car, etc. The logo looked a little like a Pac Man which was not unintentional.

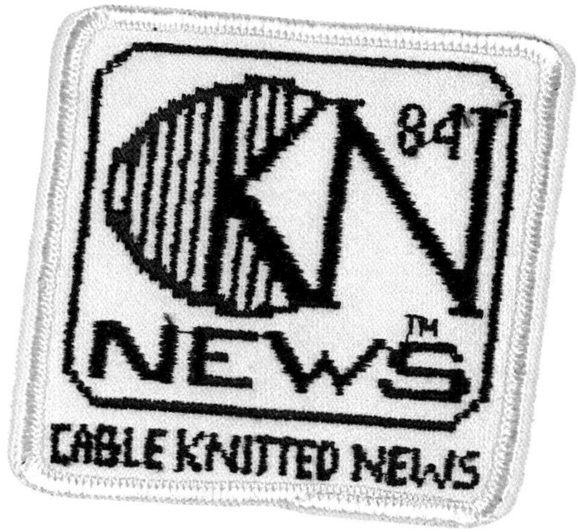

I would work by designing on an Apple computer and then the technician would translate the design to punch tape which could be read by the computer on the knitting machine. Every letter had to be constructed dot by dot, so the process was very tedious in certain ways. Pages got lost in memory and had to be reconstructed.

I played the role of Chairman of the Board, reporter, editor, and manager. We even managed to rent a UPI machine at a remarkably cheap rate so there was a receiving dish on the top of the house and a UPI machine clicking away inside the offices. I was a newsman on every level, or at least the illusion of one from my perspective.

DK Were you transforming hard news into soft news?

PS I'll happily accept that pun. That would be consistent with all the other puns which were built into this project, such as "stretching the truth," and "unraveling events of the day."

DK Or weaving a story?

PS The headlines that came from the UPI served as the substance of **Cable Knitted News.** I was just doing my job. Exaggerated puns were the norm. Some of the news pages were transformed into clothing so that you were wearing the news of the day.

DK And fashion is always news.

PS The first pages were simple, but after a while we got more creative, more visually interesting. It was difficult to use illustration. Our first pages came out when Mondale was nominated so the headline read: "Jersey pulls Fritz over the top." Our motto was: "Knot the news, Knit to fit, Unravelling Events Byte by Bit." We did about nine pages in twelve weeks. Most pages were acrylic but we knitted one of each page out of cotton for the Simkin Archives.

PS We got TV coverage, Wells Fargo Bank gave us a plaque to welcome us to the community; it was good in California.

In 1985 I was commissioned to come up with a performance project for The Gallery at Market Street East in Philadelphia. I developed **ACME, Inc.** or **"Arts and Cultural Maintenance Engineers Implementing New Creations,"** another corporate entity like **CKN**. The mall lent us a store front and we used students and visiting artists. It was a very special educational moment. The performing and plastic arts students worked together and got paid a minimum wage to boot. Their job was to be janitors. The kids who wore the **ACME, Inc.** jumpsuits would make art in the mall and record their work in photographs which we would exhibit in the store-front window. The janitorial carts contained the props and signage for the performance or installation pieces. My part in all of this was to create the concept and facilitate its implementation.

DK Does this bring us to the diner, **IFACTS?** You mentioned before that when you were trying to find a knitting machine for **CKN** you used the phone book. Could you tell me a little about the *Yellow Pages* as source material for the artist?

PS That's how I found the diner, I looked under "D" for Diner and sure enough one company in New Jersey, Kullman Industries, had an old diner that they were using for a garage. The next day I went up to look at it.

DK Why a diner?

PS Because the premise of the show was to solve the problem of the specific location, which was the University City Science Center, I decided to become my own little corporate entity or an institute for the advanced study of something; thus the creation of **IFACTS: The Institute For Advanced Creative Thoughts and Stuff.** The Science Center is a conglomerate of separate science organizations, so I created a resident organization at the Science Center which was my think tank. We needed a home and I did not want to use one of their cubicles inside. There was, however, this nice lot at the corner of 36th and Market next to the UCSC headquarters, so a diner seemed like the right solution. The diner is an archetype of an American structure and was also technologically advanced for its time; airstream design, modular, looks efficient. I didn't want a restaurant but I liked the puns about food for thought.

The diner was never done, as in "finished." I was always working on it. The premise of **IFACTS** was to invite other artists to come and be fellows and fellahs (sic) of the institute and to do their own art within that context. The spiral staircase was imported from Maine and served as a staircase to heaven, an aerial perch, a way to get up high, for a clear view of matters and it reminds one of the spiralling 'round which was part of **IFACTS:** "it is a fact if it acts as if it is a fact if it acts as if it is . . ." Inside the diner artists did proposals and idea boards which were on display. There was a story board about Art Johnny who was a detective. Then **IFACTS** led to a radio program at Moore College of Art called **IFACTS Radio.** Our motto was "In Your Air, which was a play on "on the air" and "in your ear." It was a real radio station and once again I used the *Yellow Pages* and found Low Power Broadcasting. They lent me the equipment and I set up the radio station in the window of the gallery.

DK Did **IFACTS** reflect any of your experiences at the **Luncheonette?**

PS John Formicola and I had a little luncheonette in the Italian Market in South Philadelphia some twelve

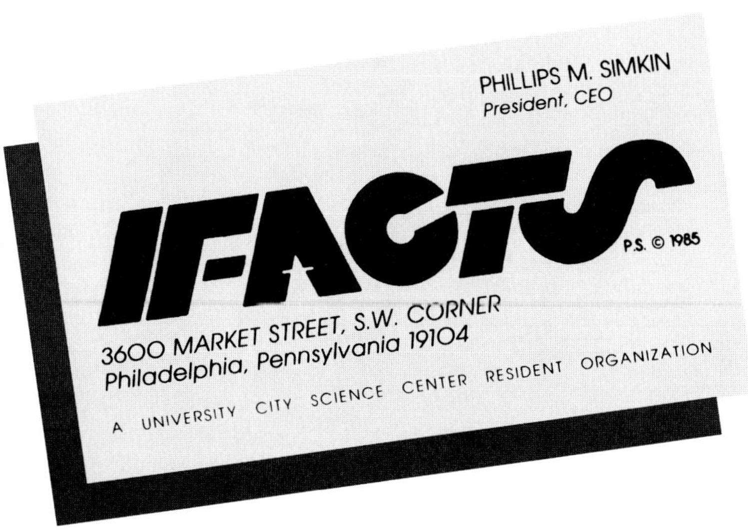

years ago. But now the diner had nothing to do with real edible food. The diner is a think tank, a catalytic center, a conference center. The diner as a structure is a humanistic element where people gathered and chatted and sat around at all hours of the day.

If I had to define **IFACTS** in the best way, it would be to call it a Trojan Horse. It came in a sense of a derelict being restored, it filled the role of a parody of the Science Center and it introduced an architectural element to the landscape. I wanted **IFACTS** to serve as a container for much more important stuff. It should serve as a sort of launching pad for artistic ideas and hopes. The diner provides a situation which is comfortable because it is familiar and unpretentious, yet provocative. It could allow you to encounter new ideas or re-think old ones.

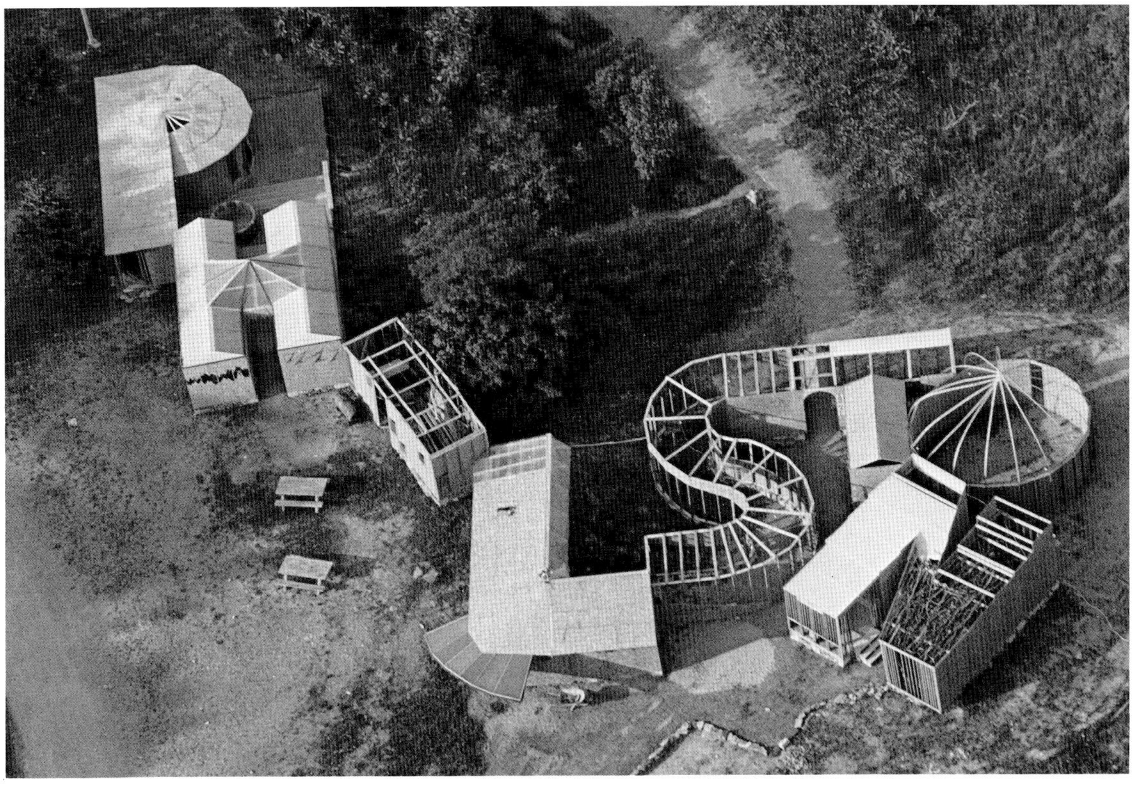

***PHILSTON, 1986,* ArtPark, Lewiston, NY. Aerial view of one acre border town on Niagara River.**

The next project is at ArtPark. I'm going to make a little town called **PHILSTON,** the "Best Little Border Town Under the Northern Sun." It is going to be the gateway to the Niagara Gorge, and it will have an unknown population. There are eight structures, almost like a wild west town stage set. I have one acre of the gorge in Lewiston. Each of the eight buildings will be one of the letters of the town's name, so that "P" is the pastry shop, "H" is the hotel, "I" is the cottage industry, "L" is the library, "S" is the general store, "T" is the town hall and tourist center, "O" is the opera and orchestra, "N" is the newspaper, and there you have **PHILSTON**. Lewiston is the American city and Queenston is the Canadian city on the other side of the Niagara River so I thought **PHILSTON** could be wedged right between the "Biggest Little Ton on the Gorge." I want to relate to the foreign nation, Canada. If I could manage, I thought a mirror town like **PHILSTON** on the Canadian side could be named Knotslip, which is almost **PHILSTON** spelled backwards.

The assumptions which are at the core of **PHILSTON** are:

A. To do a piece that could only be done at ArtPark
B. To involve the public directly in some way
C. To have visual impact
D. To be easy to assemble and disassemble

DK You seem to aim your work at a broad spectrum of the population as your audience. It rarely tends to be exotic or elitist. Rather it draws a diverse population into participation in non-threatening activities that are often based on common experiences. It is only after the event, most often, that a symbolic social comment reads through. The idea fuels the mechanism but the participation makes it complete. Thank you.

By Phil Simkin

PHILSTON, NY 1986

PHILSTON was executed while I was a Project Artist-in-Residence at ArtPark, Lewiston, NY during the month of July 1986. It was a full scale mock border town sited along the Niagara River boundary with Canada. It consisted of eight, custom built life scale (averaging 8′ tall plus roofline × 16′ × 24′ long) wooden buildings, each of which was in the shape of a letter in the town's name. **"P"** was the *PHILSTON Pleasure Palace,* and it had its own outside deck on which sat a water-filled redwood hot tub and a barbecue grill. An interior patisserie counter and stools to host occasional tasty treats were positioned under a conical roof. It had the look of a Big Sur, California cliff house. The open back wall of the **"P"** overlooked a Canadian vista across the Niagara and offered a view of the rest of **PHILSTON** as the town curved around in descending elevation towards the gorge edge. *PHILSTON Heights Hotel* had four curtained rooms with bed ensembles in each compartment of the letter **"H"**. The central lobby had a clear poly roof and chandelier while the trappings of each room varied. Public naps and late night resting sometimes took place. Each room had its own signature geometry with a variety of cut-out wall patterns. *PHILSTON Industries* was the **"I"** building and it housed the building jigs used to construct the town, along with assorted industrial age gizmos including its own 20′ water tower. The **"L"** shaped structure was the *PHILSTON Phantasy Lounge* and it functioned as a fully outfitted bush bar (it was built around a large existing prickly bush) complete with urethaned "L" shaped counter, slat benches, bar appliances, overhead fan, a counter-top window for outside road service, small tables, stools and illuminated beer signs. It was a very popular end-of-the-work-day site. *PHILSTON Souvenir Shoppe* was an outdoor display zone in a framed out letter **"S"** structure, complete with wire racks, display case and town artifacts. **"T"** stood for the *PHILSTON Town Hall* and it had an arch in the crossbar of the letter structure permitting passage through on a traditional park fisherman's route, the Lower Gorge Road, around which **PHILSTON** was sited. As helmet-clad Firechief and founding Mayor Phil of **PHILSTON** I had a working console TV at the governmental desk and a leather chair to relax in while gazing out the screened open back wall of the **"T"** towards the bridge to Canada a half-mile away. The **"O"** structure was the *PHILSTON Opera House* and it was a twenty-four foot diameter by eight foot tall cylinder with an onion domed wood slat open-air roof. An enhanced echo was always in evidence, and visitors could and did engage in spontaneous crooning and whistling. The *PHILSTON Network News* was in the **"N"** building, and it housed an editorial desk environment leading to the "N" 's diagonal corridor from which one moved to the other leg of the "N" to find dozens of old typewriters lining the walls, many filled with paper and in working condition. The public typed their thoughts which were collected in the *PHILSTON Times'* first and only issue. The whole town with its eight structures automatically lit up at night as a magical oasis out in the starry skied darkness of the ArtPark gorge.

As an expression of a self-described building and governing spirit inherent in the early American western border gateway towns such as Lewiston itself, **PHILSTON** was engaged in the business of bringing itself into existence. Four young interns, Carey, Jack, Alison and Margaret, physically built each building, and in fact designed the interiors and secondary characteristics of four to five of the structures. They and I, working alongside them, emulated a modern, mock version of the energy and strategies that had to comprise the early American ingenuity required of social and physical invention; the pioneer spirit if you will. This defined its public utility as a factor of the personalities of its builders and primary occupants. This one acre scale sweat-and-hammer-swing experience created a special 'place' in a tabula rasa public 'space' that would at summer's end, in keeping with ArtPark's and my own personal philosophy, disappear without a trace.

PHILSTON was a site relevant art solution consistent with the attributes of my **American Enterprise Series** theme, complete with all the risks and uncertainties inherent in such an ambitious, unpredictable undertaking. The process was challenging fun to solve for the Philstonians while the life scale sculptural evidence offered an unexpected and curious experience for the hundreds of park tourists throughout the summer.

Institute For Advanced Creative Thoughts and Stuff, IFACTS, 1985–1986

University City Science Center, Philadelphia, Pennsylvania. As a project commissioned by gallery director Libby Newman for their Art-in-Science V Series, I invented a mock creative think tank and artistic research nexus to be in keeping with the established philosophy and activities of the UCSC, the country's first urban science research park. To house **IFACTS,** I obtained a classic 30's diner shell from Kullman Dining car company in New Jersey and moved it to a 36th & Market Street vacant lot next to the UCSC corporate headquarters. We were listed as an official UCSC resident organization, complete with telephone extension and alphabetical listing.

Trappings associated with visually and functionally establishing this stainless steel relic as the world HQ of **IFACTS** were put in place by me over the six months of the project. I invited selected artists to be **IFACTS** "Fella's" and creative collaborators and to make their own new artworks for this shadow academic enterprise. A newly acquired thirty foot flagpole flew the official logo colors and separate festive banner (designed by John Formicola), a large letter graphic logo sign of my design sat atop the diner, a presidential parking space was established for my official company car (the only CEO in the UCSC to have one at his corporate front door) and a typical building site signboard listing atypical credits was in place throughout the restoration of the diner shell. I imported a 20′ spiral staircase from Maine to serve as a visual and functional aerial perusal perch. David Cadbury planted the corporate pumpkin patch and later an open air aviary on the adjoining lot. Peter Lister painted the classical Grecian sky on the diner's skirt.

Tom Levy obtained and programed the digital flashing bus style message display on the diner's roof. Steffi Simkin composed and recorded the official theme melody incorporated into our answer machine greeting and messages. Art Anderson, John Kosmer, Joyce Reber, Lois Johnson, Tom Porett and others contributed their graphic and written originals to the effort.

An official Bored (sic) meeting of the Bored of **IFACTS** met in plenary session in the UCSC conference room and issues of import were entertained in keeping with the official corporate motto: "It is a fact if it acts as if it is a fact if it acts as if it is . . ." Assorted gatherings including the celebration of New Years Eve, a PCA printmaking party, numerous small group conclaves and individual confabs took place inside the diner over its six month's tenure.

The interior had been undergoing a continuous state of remodeling in which I installed booths, peripatetic heat (both baseboard electric and a wood burning fireplace), and light, a CEO chairman's chair (Santa's department store throne from my reserve props department), a Bored Room table (two back to back leather doctor's examining couches ringed by diner stools), an A-Copy borrowed copy machine, electronic blackboard, an IBM typewriter, and a large supply of official **IFACTS** letterhead stationery and calling cards.

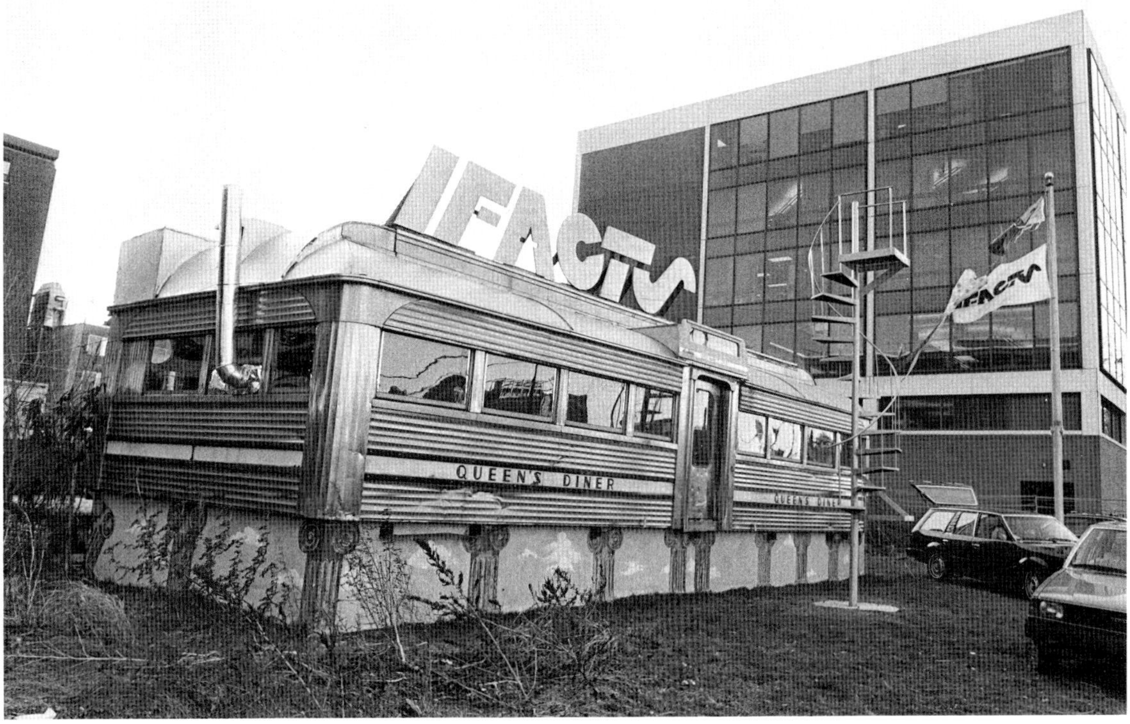

***Institute for Advanced Creative Thoughts and Stuff 1985–86,* University City Science Center, Philadelphia. Site view.**

ACME, INC. 1985, Gallery Mall, Philadelphia. View of storefront and ACME, INC. performers around escalator cart.

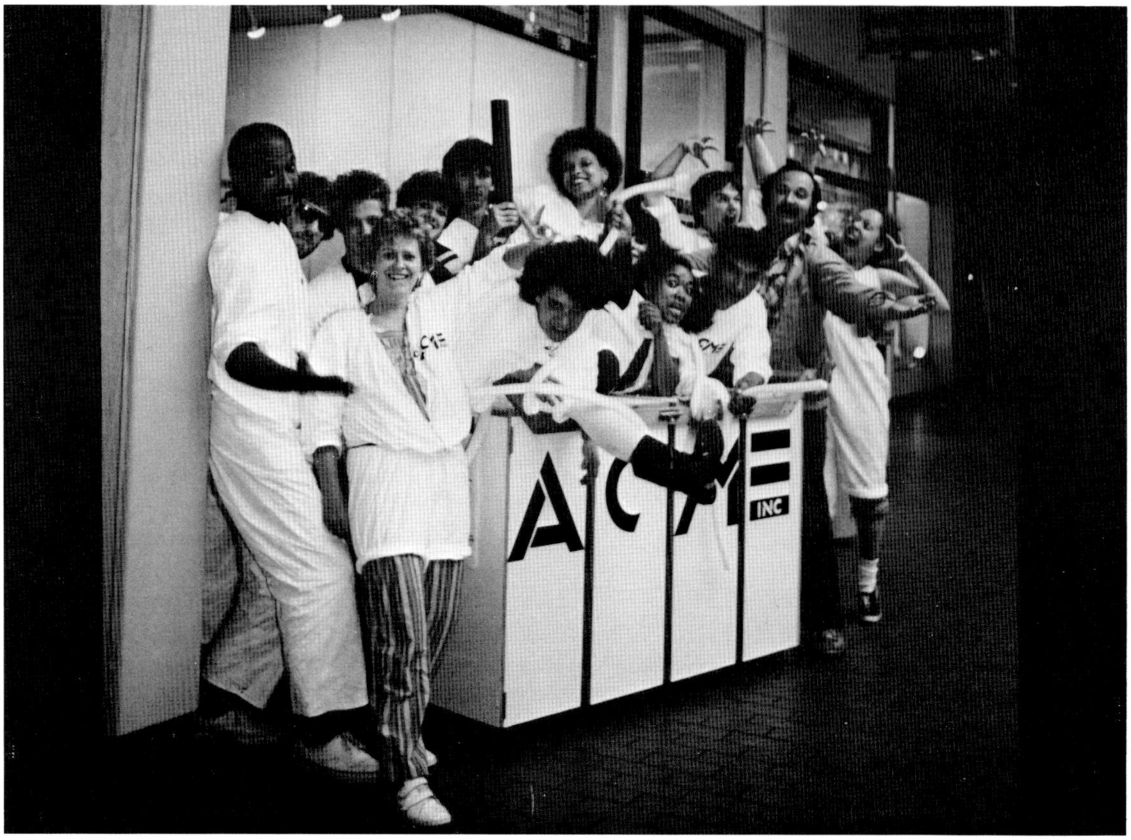

The American enterprise of Academic Research Institution business was in full mock swing. To the public passing through this busy academic university area (University of Pennsylvania and Drexel University), the idiosyncratic, enigmatic diner which had mysteriously appeared from nowhere along with its dedicated participants presented a curious attraction. The installation netted many "hello's" from the resident science community researchers and administrators, some of whom exchanged and "interfaced" with me in a collegial interaction. My **Institute For Advanced Creative Thoughts and Stuff,** with "stuff" functioning as the operative word, became a mini-crossroads of communication between the individual artist and the singular technaut.

The diner structure had to be moved at the conclusion of the project and has since been a temporary guest on several different friendly developer's lots located by the Delaware River in the Port of Philadelphia. **IFACTS,** as an oversized object and a conceptual notion, remains in flux in the best tradition of American enterprise.

Arts and Cultural Maintenance Engineers Implementing New Creations, ACME INC., 1985, The Gallery at Market East, Philadelphia, Pennsylvania. I was commissioned by the Rouse Company of Maryland coordinated by Ms. Becky Hannum, Director of their Arts in the Marketplace Program, to create a performance artwork for The Gallery which they managed. With Philadelphia Colleges of the Arts as a co-sponsor, I devised a piece that would tap the creative energies of PCA's art, music, dance and theatre students.

My premise was simply to create a business, **ACME INC.** which would have its own storefront in the mall and from which an energetic troupe of the most creative arts students could operate. In effect, they would be art janitors paid to culturally maintain and tend to America's social/commercial indoor Main Street. On a regular daily basis, for one month, it would be perfectly normal to see these youthful talents going about their creative chores in the mall venue as if on-the-hoof, ad hoc invention was a normal and expected activity right along with railing polishing, floor sweeping, and sales promotional samplings.

In order to assemble the best participants, a one week workshop I titled **ECAM (Experiential Collaborative Arts Module)** was held at PCA with Sherri Vita of the PCA faculty as Director and me as visiting artist consultant. We held school-wide auditions, selected the twenty best, exposed them to three visiting artist-teachers in one day sessions (Pat Oleszko, Chris Hodge, Manfred Fishbeck) and Sherri and I selected the final ten plus alternates to be official **ACME INC'ers.** An empty storefront was assigned to our operation by the Mall, and it served as home base, complete with phone, dressing rooms, display window, and commercial authenticity. Location, location, location! Supplies were donated by Taws Art Supply and the department stores of The Gallery. Special materials were purchased as needed, a fabricated overhead storefront sign was made, a video/still-photo documentation crew were brought on board and rapidly we were ready to begin making raw art throughout the public shopping area. I designed and had built the official **ACME INC.** segmented escalator cart, mechanically able to travel up and down on the key motive element in every mall, the escalators. It was to serve as our material resources and video equipment mobile unit.

Each morning began with a review of the previous day's accomplishments, a group discussion of the day's goals, and the handling of any problems that might come up.

A key to the success of this performance artwork was the informed management of the **ACME INC'ers,** with Sherri as project manager for this purpose. I played the role of primary project artist and made certain that the overall performance art relevance of this experiment would be professional and consistent with my own standards. The important issue in **ACME INC.** was that the students were not executing "my" art, but rather their own site-specific activities in multi-media fashion. Early on, I had replaced my personal art-making control over the daily creative activities with a skeletal conceptual framework that emphasized constructive guidance. The experiment in action here was precisely that they were on new territory as young art inventors. It was to be exclusively "their" turf and the shopping public constituted their raw ingredient and audience.

Many emotions, discoveries, some disappointments, unique psychological and social interactions and even some interesting and substantial art occurred during the month. Rules were formulated in midstream, daily self-critiques produced occasional changes in direction of the project's enactment and it was clear that the success of the venture was tied into the very unknown nature of the central creative activity itself, the making of new art. As a part of my **American Enterprise Series, ACME INC.** integrated itself easily enough into the fabric of the commercial marketplace and placed the tentative raw actions associated with youthful artmaking directly in the midst of Mr. and Mrs. Economic America.

Cable Knitted News, CKN, 1984, Capp Street Project, San Francisco, California. The Democratic National Convention was scheduled for San Francisco during the time of my stay and the Los Angeles Olympics was also to take place in late summer. These two facts, combined with my eastern seaboard perceptions of the Bay Area and California culture in general, led me to an analysis of the givens that yielded the idea to create a media conglomerate. I would address these two mega events right along with the rest of the world's fourth estate, as they and I simultaneously descended on California to report the news.

The proximity of America's computer cradle, Silicon Valley, to San Francisco, the fact that the jacquard textile loom was essentially the world's first mechanical computer device, the fashion-conscious trend setting influences that typically emanate from the West coast all coupled with my interest in creating a parodistic business venture in the spirit of American enterprise in an art gallery that already architecturally looked like a high tech venture capital operation inevitably led me to the invention of **Cable Knitted News. CKN** would knit the news on a weekly basis. What I was lacking, of course, was any knowledge about knitting or news organizations, and from three thousand miles away, the fear of failure was looming (pun intended) larger every moment.

Intensive research, telephoning and visiting produced a company, Stoll America, that would be willing to loan me a means by which to directly knit the news and it turned out to be a one hundred thousand dollar industrial electronic knitting machine, with British technician attached. Arrangements were made with United Press International to rent a state-of-the-art satellite dish wire service news machine for instant receipt of the same data that every major media operation was also simultaneously receiving.

After driving across America for the first time, searching all along the way for additional clues to my new media role at the end of the road, I arrived with vacationing friend Lois Johnson to begin installing the corporate headquarters of **Cable Knitted News.** With the help of Capp Street Project Director Anne Hatch, curator Leah Levy and preparator Scott Mertens, we constructed a multi-room media environment out of the open first floor gallery that included expensive borrowed contemporary furniture for the reception foyer, a CEO's luxurious office, a news room, a knitting manufacturing room and a sewing production area. The local Wells Fargo Bank branch at which **CKN** had its account, welcomed us to the neighborhood with a brass plaque personally inscribed and suitable for hanging in the corporate offices. Bank V.P. Larry Zanoline treated CEO Simkin with executive courtesies that clearly set the stage for my ensuing three month's role playing.

By the first day of the Democratic National Convention **CKN** miraculously was operational. The first pages were finished with details gleaned from the endless rolls of yellow paper spewing day and night from my wire service machine, and were rewritten by me with rhyming alliteration and exaggerated hyperbole. Knitting history had begun.

As the project proceeded over the twelve weeks of my artist-in-residency, the knitted pages became more sophisticated as world events were unfolding; including the Summer Olympics, a Middle East crisis, a space shuttle launch, Richard Burton's demise, a runaway cable car, sharks at Stinson Beach and **CKN's** farewell departure for the East Coast as reported by itself about itself. All these real world events provided good grist for my editorial humor mill. I "stretched the truth," "spun a few yarns," wrote a few "purls of wisdom" and generally adhered to the official **CKN** motto of: "Knot the News and Knit to Fit, Unravelling Events, Byte by Bit." We eventually knitted small variable editions of nine different pages, each three and one half feet wide and initially five but later seven to nine feet long.

In our production area, volunteer seamstresses designed and sewed wearable clothing out of some of the knitted pages. One lady made a fishwrap (reminiscent of the traditional use of newspapers), and another made a **Cable Knitted News** Corvette car bra and matching bikini top, while some legitimate high fashion pieces emerged from the hands of talented fellow volunteer artist-seamstresses. Many of the garments were later modeled for a photo opportunity in front of the gallery.

The real media soon discovered **CKN** and the Cable News Network—CNN (recognizing the call letter similarity let alone the parody) came one day to film us. I was told weeks later by a gallery visitor that he and his wife had seen us in Hong Kong on TV. I was later told that potentially sixty million subscribers worldwide saw the CNN feature. My mock media message was indeed making marks. UPI reported **CKN** as a news story and put it out over the national wire so I had the pleasure of seeing our existence being printed out over my own wire machine along with the rest of the country's media industry. And friends then heard the same news about **CKN** taken off the wire and read on New York radio and printed as a good humor news filler in newspapers nationwide.

Cable Knitted News functioned as the linchpin in my corporate role playing. I have to wonder whether the four subsequent projects in the **Series** ending with **DARING** have satiated my pleasure at momentary mock entrepreneurship. With its inherent virtue of the absence of green profit or loss responsibilities, these **American Enterprise** adventures have been filled with all the other substantive as well as fun attributes associated with business boffo. Being founding mayor of a town that bears my name, **PHILSTON, NY** had its vanity privileges. The ArtPark staff, with a twinkle in their eye, always called me "Mr. Mayor." And, turning the key to an expensive mall storefront in **ACME, INC.** with a thirty percent merchants luncheon discount at the restaurant several doors down did have its appeal.

Or have these enterprise experiences simply served to tease my appetite and set the stage for a yet invisible future journey into a serious sampling of the American Dream? I believe the **IFACTS** motto may hold a clue: "it is a fact if it acts as if it is!"

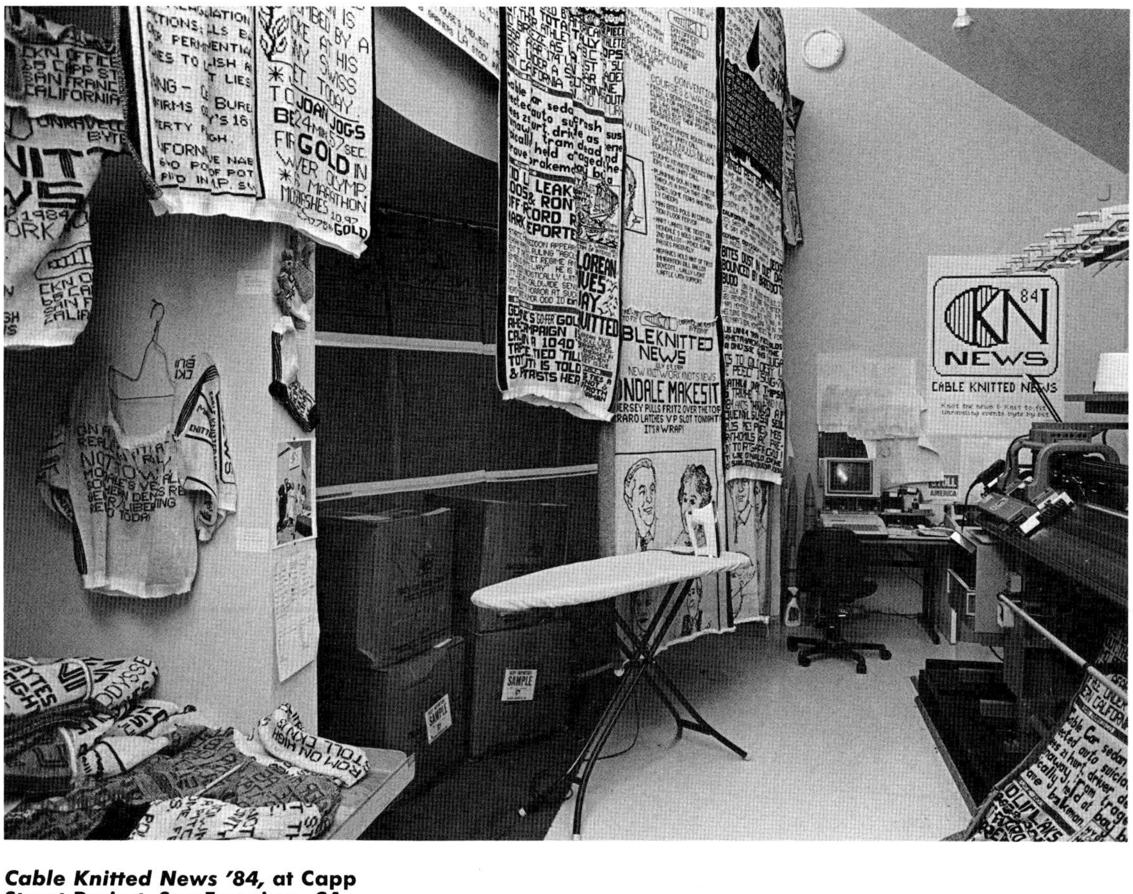

***Cable Knitted News '84*, at Capp Street Project, San Francisco, CA. Manufacturing room area of CKN project showing electronic knitting machine, computer prep area and inventory of knitted pages and one-of-a-kind garments.**

PHILLIPS SIMKIN

Birthplace: Philadelphia, PA
1944

Education:

1965	B.F.A. Tyler School of Art of Temple University, Philadelphia, PA
1967	M.F.A. Cornell University, Ithaca, NY

Academic Experience:

1973–present	Associate Professor with tenure at York College, City University of New York
1973–present	Adjunct Associate Professor at Moore College of Art, Philadelphia, PA
1970–1973	Assistant Professor, University of Maryland at College Park

Fellowships / Grants

1987	Commissioned Danceteller collaboration, **ZOMFF'87,** Pew Foundation and Reading Terminal Market
1986	NEA Special Projects Grant, Pennsylvania Council on the Arts Visual Arts Grant, The Temple Gallery, Temple University, Tyler School of Art commissioned project—**DARING**
	Natural Heritage Trust Project, Artist-in-Residence, ArtPark, Lewiston, NY
1980	National Fine Arts Committee, XIII Winter Olympics commission, Lake Placid, NY
	Pennsylvania State Arts Council Artists Grant, sculpture
1976	Creative Artists Public Service program sculpture grant, NY
1975	National Endowment for the Arts Fellowship Grant, sculpture
	Natural Heritage Trust Artist-in-Residence Grant, ArtPark, Lewiston, NY
1973	National Endowment for the Arts short-term activities grant
1970	Marjorie Heilman Visiting Artist Grant, Swarthmore College, Swarthmore, PA
1968–1969	Post Graduate Fellow in Fine Arts, University of Pennsylvania
1965–1966	Teaching Assistantship Cornell University, graduate fellowship
1961–1965	Philadelphia Board of Education Art Scholarship
1961–1965	Stella Elkins Tyler Art Scholarship, Temple University, Philadelphia, PA

Exhibitions / Projects:

Catalog Published

1987	Juried selection, City of Philadelphia, 1% for Art Program, New Criminal Justice Center commissions
1986	*Project **DARING,** The Temple Gallery, Temple University, Tyler School of Art, Philadelphia, PA
	*Project **PHILSTON,** ArtPark, Project Artist-in-Residence, Lewiston, NY
1985	*Project **IFACTS,** University City Science Center, ART-IN-SCIENCE series, Philadelphia, PA
	Project **ACME, INC,** The Gallery at Market Street East, Rouse Co. and PCA project, Philadelphia, PA
1984	*Project **Cable Knitted News,** Capp Street Project Artist-in-Residence, San Francisco, CA
1983	**Three Natural Lines,** competition-winning selection, Franklintown Corp. Art Commission, Philadelphia, PA
1982	**Rosebits,** "Sculpture 300" invitational Philadelphia Art Alliance outdoor works
	Project **Moore Pi r^2** commissioned inaugural event, Moore College of Art, Philadelphia, PA
	Project **"Sac it to 'em"** Visiting Artist University of North Dakota, Grand Forks, ND
1981	CAPS at the State Museum, New York State Museum, Albany, NY
1980	*Project **ROSEBUD II-Seven Self-Propelled Earthly Parodies,** XIII Winter Olympics, commissioned performance project, Lake Placid, NY
1979	**American Drawings II,** Smithsonian Institution Travelling Exhibition
1978	***Philadelphia Contemporary Drawing Part II,** Philadelphia Museum of Art
	WUHY public radio, live commissioned soundwork, FM band, 2 hour performance, Philadelphia, PA
	Solo exhibition/project **To a Fault . . . ,** Pennsylvania Academy of Fine Arts, Philadelphia, PA
1977	**HUMAN PUZZLE** 3rd performance, "I Love New York Festival." Albany, NY
	Art Yard Artist-in-Residence invitational project, Brooklyn Museum, Brooklyn, NY
1977	**Forms in Focus,** group outdoor exhibition, Co-op City, Bronx, NY
	Project **CHOICES (III)** JFK Plaza, '76 Bicentennial Celebration sponsored by City of Philadelphia
1976	Solo exhibition and retrospective, Marian Locks Art Gallery, Philadelphia, PA
	***Philadelphia-Houston Exchange,** Institute of Contemporary Art, University of Pennsylvania, Philadelphia, PA
	***Three Centuries of American Art,** Bicentennial Exhibition, Philadelphia Museum of Art
	Project **CHOICES (II), A Month of Sundays,** exhibition, PS 1, Long Island City, NY
	COMMODITY EXCHANGE (II) Briarcliff College Art Gallery, Briarcliff Manor, NY
1975	*Project **CHOICES** special event, Earl W. Brydges ArtPark, Lewiston, NY
	MOVE IT OR LOSE IT commissioned event 60th Anniversary, Philadelphia Print Club
	HUMAN PUZZLE, 2nd performance, Philadelphia 76 Inc., Bicentennial Commission, Philadelphia, PA
	***HUMAN PUZZLE,** 1st performance, Earl W. Brydges ArtPark, Lewiston, NY
	***COMMODITY EXCHANGE,** Earl W. Brydges ArtPark, Lewiston, NY
1974	**DISPLACEMENT PROJECT (II)** installation, West Foyer, Philadelphia Museum of Art
	***DISPLACEMENT PROJECT (I)** installation, Institute of Contemporary Art, Boston, MA
1973	***YOUR FIFTEEN MINUTES, STAIRS TO HEAVEN,** "Made in Philadelphia" exhibition, **PUBLIC CENTER FOR THE COLLECTION AND DISSEMINATION OF SECRETS,** "In Urban Sites" phase, catalog essay by Josephine Withers, Institute of Contemporary Art, University of Pennsylvania, Philadelphia, PA
1972	Solo exhibition/project, University of Maryland Art Gallery, College Park, MD
1970	Solo exhibition/project , Wilcox Art Gallery, Swarthmore College, Swarthmore, PA

Selected Bibliography:

1987 *Fiber Arts,* Jan/Feb 1987, vol. 14, no. 2 **Cable Knitted News** article

1986 *High Performance,* #36, Vol. Nine, Number 4; *New Art Examiner,* March, exhib. reviews; *Philadelphia Daily News, Philadelphia Inquirer,* AP wire feature articles, **DARING** project

Arts, November, color photo and mention, **PHILSTON** project ArtPark, NY

Philadelphia Inquirer Magazine, Jan. 26, feature article **IFACTS** project

1985 *Philadelphia Inquirer Magazine,* Jan. 6, "Our Town" column, Avery Rome essay

1984 *Artweek,* Aug. 25, 1984, critic review and photo, **Cable Knitted News** Project, San Francisco, CA, Capp Street Project

San Francisco Chronicle, Aug. 1, 1984, feature article and photo, **Cable Knitted News** Project, Capp Street Project

Chronicle of Higher Education, UP wire photo, full page, back cover, **Moore Pi r^2** event

1982 *Philadelphia Inquirer* and *Daily News,* March 23, 1982, photo and copy, **Moore Pi r^2** inaugural event performance

Grand Forks Herald, Feb. 25, 1982, photo and caption, visiting artist, project **SAC it to 'em** UND

1980 *Art in America,* April, color photo and commentary Olympic Art article

Artforum, April, color photos/commentary Olympic Art article

1979 *Inside Sports,* Vol. 1, Newsweek Inc. publisher, premier issue, Olympic Project article full page

The List, biographical summary, Independent Curators Inc., Washington, DC

Philadelphia Inquirer, Dec. 6, 1979, Olympic **ROSEBUD** Project "People" page feature article

1978 *Art in America,* November, Exhibition review

Philadelphia Bulletin, June 4, Art Review

1977 *Artnews,* April, review of solo exhibition

Philadelphia Magazine, article on **Buck-a-Lick** event, ICA

ArtPark 76, catalogue inclusion, Project Artist-in-Residence summer

Visual Art 1976–1977, catalogue, Creative Artists Public Service Program Grant, NY

The Sunday Bulletin, Jan. 16, Art Review

Philadelphia Inquirer, Jan., Art Review

1976 *Philadelphia Inquirer,* Dec. 18, Metro Page and column (UP-wirephoto)

In Urban Sites, **Choices Project** series newsprint broadside mailer, Institute for Art and Urban Resources, NY

Soho News, Oct. 7, photo illustration, PS 1 **Month of Sundays** exhibition, **Choices Project**

Buffalo Courier-Express, Aug. 16, article **Choices Project** at ArtPark

1975 *Artforum,* October edition, **Chairs Project,** photo in Robert Morris article

Buffalo Courier-Express, Aug. 13, article **Commodity Exchange Project** ArtPark, N Y

Niagara Gazette, Aug. 9, photo spread, **Human Puzzle** ArtPark, NY

1974 *The Evening Bulletin,* Dec. 4, "Metro" feature article, **Displacement Project II,** pinhole camera installation, Philadelphia Museum of Art, Philadelphia, PA

The Christian Science Monitor, April 23, article, **Displacement Project 1,** Boston ICA, Boston, MA

1973 *Philadelphia Inquirer,* Vol. 288, no. 140, front page feature article and AP wire, **Public Center for the Collection and Dissemination of Secrets,** ICA and 30th Street Amtrak Station, Philadelphia, PA

Lectures:

1985 WHYY "Fresh Air" interview; 900 AM Talk Radio interview; UCSC exhibition **IFACTS** Project

1984 Cable News Network (CNN) and Westinghouse Broadcast System (KPIX-5) **CKN** News Project feature; SUNY Purchase NEA artists lecture series; Philadelphia College of Art; University of Vermont, Burlington, VT, Art Department Lecture Series; San Jose State; San Francisco State; Capp Street Project Artist Lecture Series

1980 Radio interview, "Choosing the Future" series, WUHY-FM Philadelphia, WBAI-FM New York, Interview and 3 minute segment; CBS TV Network, Syndicated interview and 5 minute segment; NBC Syracuse, interview; National Public Radio; Mexican TV Network; WNYC-TV, Olympic Archives; Fort Worth Film Productions, Inc.

1977 "Education of Artists Conference," Spring Hill Center, Wyazata, Minnesota

Premier, "New Arts, New Artists" TV Pilot, interview and projects reenactment

Graduate Planning Seminar: Lecture Series Tyler School of Art, Temple University

WUHY FM Public Radio, 1 hour interview

1976 Channel 3 Evening News—**Choices Maze** at JFK Plaza

WGR TV, Channel 2; Buffalo Evening News, ArtPark site, **Choices Project**

1975 Channel 10 TV, live minicam coverage of **Move It or Lose It** event, Philadelphia